# THE MIRROR OF TURQUOISE LAKE

# THE MIRROR OF TURQUOISE LAKE

Plays from the
Classical Tibetan Buddhist Tradition

An Unabridged Translation by
## TENZIN CHONYI
AND
## ROBERT HULTON-BAKER

RINCHEN PUBLICATIONS
KINGSTON, NEW YORK, USA

Published by:
Rinchen, Inc.
20 John Street
Kingston, NY 12401
(845) 331-5069
www.rinchen.com

First Edition; October, 2008

ISBN: 978-0-9714554-6-7

# Contents

## Translators' Acknowledgements

The translators gratefully acknowledge the original financial support that made this project possible which came from three Fellowship Awards by PSC-CUNY of the City University of New York. Robert Hulton-Baker thanks CUNY College of Staten Island, the Department of English, Speech, and World Literature, and the Department of Performing and Creative Arts, as well as the following individuals who assisted with scholarship, valuable insight, and editing: Dzogchen Ponlop Rinpoche, Bardor Tulku Rinpoche, Khenpo Karthar Rinpoche, Lekshe Chonyi, Jamspal, the late Terry Clifford, Arthur Mandelbaum, Edward Margolies, Ed Hack, Les Keyser, and Amy Soppet. In addition Robert Hulton-Baker is grateful for the understanding of his wife, Margaret. Tenzin Chonyi thanks Mary Rafftery for her support in text preparation.

## Acknowledgements by the Publisher

First and foremost I would like to thank Tenzin Chönyi and Robert Hulton-Baker for their fine scholarship and inspiration in producing these translations. It is especially appropriate to honor Tenzin Chönyi at this point, since his many long years of service to his teacher, His Holiness the 16th Gyalwa Karmapa, in developing Karma Triyana Dharmachakra—His Holiness' seat in the West—have recently come to fruition in the historic first visit of His Holiness Ogyen Trinley Dorje, the 17th Karmapa. Robert Hulton-Baker's illuminating introduction brings together a lifetime of practical and scholarly experience in the field of drama with his specialized study of Tibetan drama and of Buddhism in general. The unique combination of qualities and background that these two translators brought to the project has yielded a unique result in terms of quality and accessibility of their work. Robert in particular has also been most helpful with the many details of producing the book you see before you, providing significant support for its completion.

Additionally, I am very thankful to both Tenzin and Robert for their great patience and forbearance in waiting through the many delays that came up in the publication of this book.

In the production of the book itself, Florence Wetzel contributed greatly to the final editing of the manuscript. Naomi Schmidt did the beautiful cover design and page layout work, and artist Wendy Harding produced the superlative original line drawings throughout. Lama James Kukula graciously allowed his thangka painting of Thangtong Gyalpo, the founder of Tibetan drama, to be photographed for the cover. Thanks to Wendy Harding for taking the photograph. This thangkha was painted by KTD's venerable painter-in-residence, Thinley Chöjor. Sadly, Thinley Chojor passed away in April of this year. The appearance of his work in this form is a testament to the enduring legacy of his extensive artistic output, and I would also like to see it as an expression of the great love, respect, and gratitude all of us in the KTD community feel for Thinley.

Finally, I am extremely grateful to my Dharma brother and long-time supporter of Rinchen Publications, Cralle Hall, for providing the major financial backing for the production of *The Mirror of Turquoise Lake*.

I have overseen all the details of the production of this book, and take full responsibility for whatever errors or shortcomings remain.

May this book fulfill its purpose in the minds of its readers, which is to inspire us by taking us on a journey of imagination through the profound and dramatic events of the lives of great practitioners of Buddhadharma. In keeping with that inspiration, may we all give rise to the peerless outlook of bodhicitta, and follow in their example of enlightenment.

David McCarthy
President
Rinchen Publications
Kingston, New York
October, 2008

# Introduction
## BY ROBERT HULTON-BAKER

## The Origins of Tibetan Drama

The establishment of traditional Tibetan drama is attributed to the great 14th century yogi, Thangtong Gyalpo (1385-1510), who was considered an emanation of the deity Chenrezig (Avalokiteshvara in Sanskrit), the embodiment of compassion. A renowned teacher, Thangtong Gyalpo expounded Buddhist teachings and built stupas in Tibet and Bhutan. He is also known for devising and constructing suspension bridges built with hand-forged chains.

According to tradition, his bridge building inspired the creation of Tibetan Buddhist drama, known as *a-che lhamo*. During construction of one of the bridges, demonic obstruction from seven demons (known as the Seven Brothers Tsen) disrupted further progress. Thangtong Gyalpo produced a diversion, instructing seven men to dance dressed as fishermen and hunters, distracting the demons, removing the obstacles, and allowing construction to resume.

These performances also became a resource for Thangton Gyalpo to fund his bridge projects, while developing what became lhamo. According to Lobsang Dorje,[1] the earliest production of lhamo under the direction of Thangtong Gyalpo

featured songs by seven sisters from a well-to-do family who represented celestial goddesses. They praised the beauty of the local region, its mountains, meadows, fragrant junipers, and melodious songbirds. The performers also danced, accompanied in song by the famous yogi himself. Then Thangtong Gyalpo gave a Buddhist teaching, followed by a group recitation of the mantra, OM MANI PEME HUNG. Later, the audience was invited to give aid to the bridge-building project.

Over time lhamo became popular and eventually began to incorporate biographies known as *namthar*. Traditional lhamo has nine namthar of classical origin plus a tenth composed more recently.[2] These stories became an essential part of Tibetan lhamo, inspired by a variety of sources including Tibetan Buddhist histories, hagiographies, popular tales, and narratives from the Pali Buddhist folk canon (*Jataka Tales*). For example, *Songtsen Gampo*, a namthar originating from Tibetan history, centers on the reign of Tibet's first Buddhist King. Narratives are based on fabulous or miraculous events, such as *Drowa Zangmo*, the tale of a dakini who protects her children by descending from a heavenly world in the shape of animals. Other plots can be traced to folk custom, as in *Nangsa Wöhbum*, which presents a view of feudal culture.

Productions of lhamo by monasteries and lay troupes were often performed during holiday festivals. Lhamo is also known as Tibetan Opera and Harvest Festival Drama, named for the period in September when it was often performed. Threaded with dance, mime, and comic interludes, the textual art and performance craft of lhamo supported and complemented religious festivities. As the popularity of lhamo increased, religious and secular traveling troupes and local residents of Tibetan towns and religious centers performed lhamo for days before large audiences which included monastic and civil authorities. Funding sources for these productions varied, with traveling and local troupes supported by donations, government subsidies, or patronage from a wealthy family or monastery. Monasteries often had their own troupes, using monks as performers.

Traditional lhamo were presented regularly until the Chinese occupation of Tibet in 1959. Refugee committees of monks and lay people continue to perform lhamo in Europe, North America, Nepal, Sikkim, Bhutan, and in Dharamsala and other places in India with Tibetan refugee communities. The Tibetan group Chaksam-pa has performed lhamo in the United States, and beginning in the 1980s, performances by the Sholpa Lha-Ma group have occasionally taken place in Lhasa, the Tibetan capital.

## Traditional Productions of Lhamo

Traditionally lhamo is produced outdoors in a rectangular space on flat, open ground around a four-sided canopy erected in the center of the performance area. Within the canopy, a table holds an image of Thangtong Gyalpo before the canopy's central post. In front of the table are the seven types of traditional

Tibetan Buddhist offerings: water, rice, cymbals, incense, butter lamp, scented water, and fruit. Nearby is a wooden chest decorated on four sides to symbolize auspiciousness. Two similarly decorated chests are filled with wheat and butter meal. Nearby is another auspicious ornament, a large bottle of *chang* (barley beer). Around this setting, performers sing and dance accompanied only by cymbals and drums.

As in classical Indian drama, the physical elements of the production are simple: no front curtain, little or no standing scenery, and minimal props. Various positions on the stage establish the drama's characters in different locations, sometimes at great distances. The miming of walking or riding represents travel, and time is a fluid element unconstrained by the conventional limitations of time and place observed in classical European drama. Speeches and dialogue are sung and accompanied by dance, except for comic scenes.

Ritual embellishments lengthened lhamo festival productions to a period of several days. Traditionally, the first session begins on the first morning with a dance by seven performers dressed as fishermen. After reciting prayers to Thangtong Gyalpo, they perform the ngöndro (foundation or groundbreaking) dance. Then two men perform in the ancient *gyalu* (hunter) costume, characterized by a huge hat. Depending on the size of the company, the *gyalu* may number as many as ten dancers. Next come the *rignga*, five women dressed in brocade who dance and sing and later join with the men. The first dance by the rignga begins with a series of leaps around the performance area, as well as recitations of prayers to Thangtong Gyalpo and beings in the heavens and the *naga* realms of the lakes and seas, and finally, prayers are recited to placate demons. At the conclusion of the invocational dance, the performers make one circuit of the playing area together while dancing and singing. This prelude consumes approximately one and one-half to two hours; then, after an intermission, the namthar begins.

The performance outline is the same for each namthar. Actors sing the dialogue framed by narrative recited quickly by one of the two leaders, together known as the teacher (*lhamo gegen*) or narrator (*shung shangken*). Performances in the Dalai Lama's summer palace included a commentator who sat aside and read the narration but did not participate in supporting roles. In other places one performer leads and also acts, and the first session begins with singing and dancing by the ensemble. The gegen reads the narrative introduction to the namthar, and as the plot begins, he calls out the first character.

Solemn scenes within the lhamo are sometimes interspersed with farcical interludes performed by minor characters such as royal ministers, astrologers, monk-bodyguards, and ferrymen. These comic scenes take place within the plot or in improvised scenes such as wrestling matches, business transactions, comic arguments, or spoofs of local officials in attendance. Occasionally, spectators and performers directly engage in brief humorous exchanges in local dialect.

*Drimay Kunden* provides an example of how a lhamo usually progresses. The story is drawn from the "Vessantara," No. 547 in the Pali *Jataka Tales*, which relates stories of the Buddha's previous incarnations. It illustrates the compassion and generosity of Prince Drimay Kunden, who was exiled by his father as punishment for giving away the kingdom's most prized gem, the *cintamani*, wish-granting jewel, to a beggar. The first character announced is the father-king with his retinue of queens, servants, and ministers. As the gegen reads, the performers conclude their dance and return unobtrusively to a tent at the edge of the playing area to change costumes for later roles. A typical procession, as in *Drimay Kunden*, includes a minister who prepares the spectators for the entrance of the king. The drums and cymbals sound three times, and at the third repetition the king appears in the middle of his retinue. The king and court prostrate before the Dalai Lama or the high lama attending the performance, and the gegen begins to recite the narrative. The king and his retinue dance, and at the conclusion the king sings his lines and ends his scenes with a brief dance, after which the gegen continues the narration. The alternation of dialogue plus dance and narration is repeated throughout the performance. The lhamo concludes with prayers offered for the benefit of all sentient beings.

## Aesthetic Values in Tibetan Buddhist Drama

Lhamo also reflects classical Indian aesthetics, as well as Buddhist tantra and the bodhisattva doctrine of the mahayana tradition. The values and practices governing structure and characterization in lhamo were influenced by classical Indian aesthetics found in *kavya* literature. A major form of classical literature in Sanskrit, kavya was employed in the court epics and poetry of India from the early centuries C.E. and was a vigorous force generating works devoted to art rather than teaching (*sastra*). Evidence of Tibetan employment of kavya is supported by Dundin's Tibetan translation of the Indian commentary, *Kavya Ardashya* (*Mirror of Kavya*).

Kavya is divided into two general topics: poetics, which employs figures of speech, stanzaic forms, and other elements common to expressive aesthetic composition, and dramaturgy, which is focused on *rasa* or aesthetic "taste," the personal audience experience defined in the *Natyasastra*[3] as an indispensable element of drama.[4] The combined effect of these two elements was *priti*, delight, deemed more effective than poetics and rasa separately.

The eight basic rasas are love, humor, energy, anger, fear, grief, disgust, and astonishment. Later commentators added others, including the calmed and the heroic. The audience anticipated "tasting" the emotions reflected in the actors' performances, but actors were not expected to produce the true emotions in themselves; rasas were instead experienced through the characters' actions and dialogue. Structured around kavya principles, didactic and moral values derived

from Hinduism and Buddhism were forged in the dramaturgical fires of plot and conflict. The primary rasas of energy and the heroic are tasted by witnessing the dramatic actions of a culture-hero or saint.

Tibet employed a more limited palette of rasas than India. The most common rasas in Tibetan lhamo are love, especially of family, energy, grief, humor, as well as the heroic and the calmed. The love rasa is not always positive, as demonstrated when Nangsa discovers that the attachment of worldly love is the source of much of her unhappiness, binding her to everyday relationships and preventing her entry into a life of ascetic yogic practice. In the play, scenes of love take place in the manse garden between Nangsa and her husband and also when Nangsa confesses her love for her son, her final obstacle to entering the life of a solitary tantric yogini. This rasa underlies much of the play's sensitive and powerful poetic imagery.

The love rasa is also observed in numerous scenes in *Drimay Kunden*. This is clear at the outset of the play as Drimay Kunden's mother and father express love for their only child. As Drimay departs his native kingdom of Bheta in exile, his mother, wife, and children profess their love for him. Lengthy scenes express the sense of loss felt by his parents and children in moments of parting. Love is also mutually expressed in the conclusion when the family is happily reunited. The love rasa enhances the aesthetic impact of the play by the polarity of love's positive and negative emotional effects.

Lhamo possesses other distinguishing aesthetic characteristics. The genre demonstrates a range of Buddhist principles and practices, providing exemplary lessons. Plot development is episodic and linear, and resolutions conform to heroic comedy. Tibetan dramatic principles reflect the traditional Indian preference for individual scenes in place of a unified plot, with these scenes giving an opportunity to present a single rasa while secondarily advancing the plot.

For example, *Songtsen Gampo* contains scenes that illustrate disparate moments in the life of the king who was instrumental in establishing Buddhism in Tibet. The first scene is the most incongruous, focusing on the king's traditionally accepted role as the one who imported a method for transcribing spoken Tibetan by adapting the Sanskrit alphabet. There is no further reference to this event and it has no impact on the plot, yet the scene is incorporated into the play to introduce the king and his minister Gar (who later becomes the major character), and to illustrate Songtsen Gampo's cultural contributions to Tibet. The balance of the play concerns events leading to the betrothal of two Buddhist princesses from Nepal and China who later became Songtsen Gampo's wives and strongly influenced his conversion to Buddhism. Later, a scene of comic moments during Gar's visit to China illustrates the development of a single rasa, humor.

## Buddhism and Lhamo

Although Tibetan lhamo reflects the social, psychological, and moral values of Tibetan culture held over a span of centuries, Buddhism was the most important influence in shaping that society and influencing personal ideals. Lhamo's emphasis on Buddhist values is another example of the influence of the Indian aesthetic tradition, namely the *Natyasastra* endorsement of works of art that support a society founded on the principles of morality and ethics. Tibetan culture and its drama follow the mahayana school of Buddhism, with central emphasis on the bodhisattva vow, the commitment to achieve Buddhist enlightenment for the benefit of all sentient beings. The Tibetan Buddhist tantric (vajrayana) tradition, inseparable from the mahayana tradition, teaches that enlightenment can be achieved in a single lifetime and that all experience may be transformed into spiritual insight.

Reflections of these views are found in lhamo like *Drimay Kunden*, where Buddhist right action based on mahayana and tantric ideals attain a heroic outcome. Characters in namthar uphold these values when challenged by dramatic conflict, and the supporting characters' redemptive transformations demonstrate the positive effects of the hero's actions. Prince Drimay Kunden, for instance, exemplifies the mahayana bodhisattva vow to renounce the absolute bliss of nirvana until all sentient beings are liberated from samsaric suffering. Drimay Kunden acts solely for the benefit of others, even giving his eyes to a blind man who begs for them, thereby spiritually advancing those who witness his unshakable compassion and generosity.

Although the account of Drimay Kunden's compassionate activity is also found in Southern classic Indian Buddhist literature (the *Jataka Tales'* rendition of Prince Vessantara), the embellishments that fill and illuminate *Drimay Kunden* are characteristic of Northern Buddhism, particularly in the Tibetan references to tantra, the bodhisattva vow, and the employment of holy lamas for efficacious prayer. In contrast with the *Jataka Tales*, Drimay Kunden is suffused with Buddhist devotion and dedication such as Mande Zangmo's prayers for a son, her religious dream employing mahayana symbols, the patriarch Sakyong Dakpepal's prayers for Drimay Kunden's conception, his father's initial indulgence in Drimay's appeal for compassionate activity, and Drimay's exceptional generosity.

Prince Drimay Kunden's vow is the mahayana vow of the bodhisattva, who will not waiver as he pursues his goal of enlightenment. Elements of tantra and references to multiple deities in *Drimay Kunden* are further signs of the mahayana's impact upon this namthar. Pre-Buddhist elements arise in the appearance of Brahma and his heavenly emanations as well as the play's setting in the kingdom of Bheta in ancient India. Culturally, there is no conflict in the appearance of the Hindu deity, Brahma, because Buddhist tantric tradition sometimes either adapted or translated the Indian tantric deities, thereby continuing an ancient tradition

while adapting to Buddhist ends.

Nangsa Wöhbum's dissatisfaction with marriage is a further example of the mahayana recognition of the unsatisfactory nature of the emotional dependency on mundane life, including attachment to loved ones. Both Drimay Kunden and Nangsa Wöhbum leave behind those closest to them, their spouses, children, and parents, while at the same time retaining their love for them. Though this may appear unfeeling, the mahayana view is that these relationships can foster attachments which impede enlightenment. As the Tibetan abbot Venerable Khenpo Karthar Rinpoche remarked, "One may be bound by a chain of iron or by a chain of gold, but in either case one is not free."

Instead of being bound by just a few loving relationships, the mahayana view encourages compassion and loving kindness toward all sentient beings. In *Drimay Kunden*, virtuous acts including the hero's vow of generosity and compassion are essential elements in the bodhisattva vow to work for the enlightenment of all sentient beings. His mother and father's homage to various deities lends credence to the tantric outlook. Moreover, Drimay Kunden ultimately accepts the loss of loved ones and material possessions. These themes are also found in *Nangsa Wöhbum*, where the bodhisattva vow to achieve enlightenment is evident in Nangsa's insight into the unsatisfactory nature of the mundane and her subsequent decision to leave her marriage and enter retreat. Although Nangsa has greater difficulty leaving her family than Drimay Kunden, her eventual renunciation is similar to Drimay Kunden's recognition of the inevitable parting from loved ones. Also, her achievement of yogic *siddhi* is based on the tantric belief that success in practice awards the practitioner with exceptional qualities, as illustrated by Nangsa and her guru's ability to fly through the air.

## The Role of the Hero in Lhamo

Self-discovery in protagonists is significant in much of classical European drama, but it is not important in Indian and Tibetan kavya-inspired literatures, which do not employ a change of insight in the leading character. In Greek tragedy, Oedipus' ethical and physical transformation arises from his self-discovery of his earlier deeds of patricide and incest. In Shakespeare, tragedy can produce significant alteration of self-awareness or state of mind, as in the suicide of Othello and the madness of Lear. As in all drama, lhamo employs conflict and unexpected situations, but here the hero or heroine's state of mind is clear, certain, and stable; there is no need for the tragic discovery, confession, and expiation that occurs in classical Western drama.

If the plot in lhamo generates momentary havoc for a hero or heroine, this does not discourage the acceptance of an absolute transcendent order and values understood by performers and audience alike. In this respect, what is true for lhamo audiences was also true for Indian audiences entertained by

kavya-based poetry, drama, and epics. Plot evolution leads to the full flowering of the hero's character as the obstacles encountered stir audience interest. Drimay Kunden does not change; the conflicts and difficulties he encounters are the consequences of his refusal to reduce his personal values. Nangsa Wöhbum's resolute purpose also produces conflict and stress, but ultimately her single-mindedness enables her transcendence of immediate circumstances and the fulfillment of her goal. In minor characters, the significant change is the change of heart associated with genuinely putting Buddhist principles into practice, and this transformation comes about through the influence of the resolute behavior of the main characters.

Two factors strongly influenced plot resolution: karma (moral causation) and reincarnation, beliefs held by both Hindus and Buddhists. In kavya-influenced drama, karma dictates that the outcome of events conclude according to the correctness of a character's actions, while reincarnation offers the possibility that the death of a hero is only a pause in the evolution to another heroic and presumably more accomplished life. In some kavya literature, as in *Nangsa Wöhbum*, "false death" takes place: the resurrected heroine returns to life and is ethically positioned to more ably complete her purpose.

In the absence of a heroic tragic flaw, the Tibetan Buddhist values that appear in lhamo differ from the classical Greek tragic vision. Here, the vigor of the Tibetan protagonist creates a resolution similar to European Renaissance tragicomedy. Detachment from mundane preoccupation enables the hero to triumph, often in the face of overwhelming adversity. For instance, Drimay Kunden, born a prince and cast into exile by the political consequences arising from his generosity, overcomes hardship through further practice of compassion and altruism, and finally assumes his father's throne.

*Nangsa Wöhbum* validates Brahma's pronouncement in the *Natyasastra* that drama should support the depiction of virtuous actions and the practice of restraint.[5] The heroine follows a virtuous course first in submitting to her family's injunction to marry, and later in suffering her husband and her sister-in-law's abuse. She transcends these difficulties through her quest for instruction in Buddhist devotional practice. Evidence of her virtuous action is supported by frequent tests of Nangsa's character, confirming the wisdom of her choice. Her success is witnessed by her family, her husband, and, in the version presented in this text, his army, all of whom witness her flight into the sky.

## Lhamo Today

Despite the current challenge of keeping Tibetan culture authentic and vital, lhamo continues to be performed to edify and delight its audiences. Tibetan Buddhist dramatic opera remains a cultural testament to the religion, philosophy, and time-honored lifestyle of the people of Tibet, while offering a revealing view of

the unique Tibetan way of life. May those who read these plays be absorbed by the heroic events presented, and edified by the Buddhist principles that motivate their characters.

# Nangsa Wöhbum

## Narrator's Prologue

### THE INVOCATION: *Namo Guru Dewa Dakini!*[1]

O skillful and compassionate one, born into the Shakya lineage,[2] unvanquished by others, destroyer of maras,[3] body majestic as golden Mount Sumeru, King of the Shakyas, at your feet I prostrate.[4]

In the potala[5] of the supreme abode, emanating from the green TAM[6] light that liberates beings, mother of all the buddhas,[7] to you I prostrate.

I vow to teach all beings in their own tongue, in that of gods and demigods, in the language of nagas,[8] scent-eaters,[9] and humans, in as many sounds and languages as there may be. Our skillful and compassionate teacher[10] turned the Wheel of Dharma[11] three times. He taught the 84,000 teachings of Dharma,[12] and fittingly tamed the minds of beings.

Here are tales and legends for those like me who cannot understand the spiritual teachings, tales of birds and zombies, stories of the monkey Hanuman, King Gesar and others. Also among them are legends of King Ramana, the goddess Yitrogma, Dharma King Drimay Kunden, and more.

The Dharma teachings from the many commentaries of the vinaya are found in these tales.

Today many important leaders and ordinary people from throughout the kingdom have gathered to see this event, this spiritual offering. The life story of Nangsa Wöhbum will be performed to turn the selfish away from worldly matters and focus the mind on the Dharma. There are a number of versions of this story, including one where Nangsa is born in a heavenly form and another where Nangsa is born in a human form. On this occasion, we will present the story of the very noble dakini, the beautiful Nangsa Wöhbum, born in human form. We ask all to listen carefully.

## Narration

This story takes place here in Tibet in Upper Nari Korsum, which has three districts. Of these three districts, six mountain ranges overlook the lower region. In the middle part known as Ü and Tsang are four regions. Among these in the northeast is a village called Nyangtö Gyaltse. Near this place was Nangsa's home, Jangpekü Nangpa. There in a commoner's household lived her father, Kunzang Dechen, and her mother, Nyangtsa Saldrön. This couple faithfully recited prayers to the Goddess Green Tara day and night. By the power of completing the recitation of 100,000 of these prayers, one night Nangsa's mother experienced a number of marvelous dreams. She saw the body of the goddess as the body of all the victorious buddhas. In her dream Nyangtsa Saldrön prostrated respectfully to this emanation of the Green Forest Tara, and recognized that she was joined in karma as companion to the Goddess for her entire life.

When she woke, she went to her husband, Kunzang Dechen, and said,

"O great father, listen to me. While
sleeping last night, I experienced
an amazing and singular dream.
In the heavenly realm of Yulokö,[13]
on a precious and resplendent conch shell
throne surrounded by all the protector deities of          the
three times,[14] the heart of the Victorious Mother Tara glowed with the
green syllable TAM. Its light entered the aperture in the crown of my
head, and moving down my central channel, dissolved into my heart.
On my body grew a lotus flower. To this the dakinis made offerings,

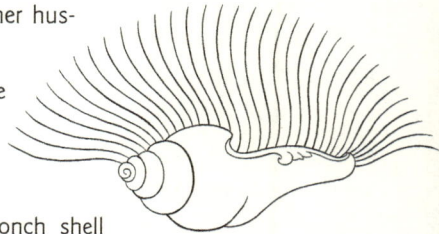

and from all directions a swarm of bees gathered, taking nectar from the lotus stamen. I surely know the dream is favorable, but Father, please interpret its significance."

Kunzang Dechen was very happy with this news, and answered: "Companion of many lifetimes, O beautiful lady, great Nyangtsa Saldrön, listen to me. Though dreams are illusory and unreal, yet this one augurs strongly for the future. The ray of light that issued from the heart syllable of the Lady Tara, the divine mother of all the victorious ones,[15] was absorbed into your heart center, and this is a sign that the blessings of Tara have entered your heart. The lotus that appeared suddenly on your body reveals that the child who is to be born from your body is the noblest of all dakinis. The gathering of bees from all directions to savor the pollen in its anthers is an omen that both pure and impure beings that need to be tamed will be helped by the activities of her body, speech, and mind. Likewise, you will have the opportunity to serve all beings through your body, speech, and mind.

"Although in our youth, in our time of white teeth, we did not have a son, now in old age, in our time of white hair, we will have a daughter. She who is born will be far better than a son; this is certain. Therefore prayers and offerings in all the eight directions should be performed. Your dream is good, Nyangtsa Saldrön! Kunzang Dechen's mind is content."

Having spoken, he made offerings upward to the Supreme Jewels,[16] and sent gifts downward to the poor. To those in the middle, monks and nuns, he offered generous service.

By the power of these prayers and virtuous actions, their child was born at the time of the waxing moon during the gathering of the dakinis, on a Thursday while the Victory Star was shining, on the auspicious tenth day of the month of the Monkey,[17] in the Male Earth Horse year.[18] Immediately after birth the child threw her mother's first milk into space as a gift. Joining her hands together in prayer, the child spoke:

"I prostrate to the Divine Mother Tara, you who have given birth to the

victorious ones throughout the three times. O Venerable Lady Tara, I make offerings and perform prostrations. I am here to benefit the beings on this earth. May all be auspicious! May the light radiating from my actions extend in all directions, establishing hundreds of thousands of beings on the path of Dharma."

Thus she spoke.

With these prayers in mind, they named the child Nangsa Wöhbum,[19] and the people of the region agreed with one voice that it should be so. Her growth was greater in one month than that of other children in a year. With her beautiful body and tranquil mind, she grew more goddesslike than human. Her parents were delighted, and they spoke in praise of their daughter in this way: "As a child of excellent lineage, she is a good girl to her father. As a fair lady born, she is a good girl to her mother. Singular among others, she is a crowning ornament to gods and humans both."

"O daughter, Nangsa Wöhbum, listen to us. All the fine-looking objects of this world we offer as one to you in praise of your beautiful goddess body. Just seeing your loveliness brings us happiness. The *kalapinka*,[20] the sparrow, the cuckoo, all these birds sing beautifully, yet none can equal the voice of Brahma; likewise, to hear your voice brings happiness. Accordingly, we give praise to your melodious voice, O Nangsa! You offer respect to the lama and the pure objects of refuge, to all beings especially loving. As a parent, just the thought of you brings joy. I give praise to your mind, O Nangsa. In the family of the loud-voiced donkey you are the quiet brown mule; in the family of the common black cow you are the beautiful white dzo.[21] That we two old ones, your parents, should have a goddess like yourself born into our family is truly wonderful."

Thus they spoke.

To her parents Nangsa replied:

"I prostrate to Tara, the Divine Mother of all the Sages.[22] Please listen to me, my dear parents. I, the girl Nangsa, surely have parents outer, inner, and secret. My outer father is Kunzang Dechen; my mother, kindness itself, is Nyangtsa Saldrön. My inner father is Chenrezig, my mother Lady Tara, white and blue. My secret father is the Supreme Stage of Great Bliss, my secret mother the Wisdom of Luminosity and Emptiness conjoined. To all my parents, outer, inner, and secret, culminating in the union of emptiness and bliss in all aspects, I respectfully prostrate."

Nangsa offered praise and prostrations both day and night, reciting

endlessly the six-syllable prayer to Avalokiteshvara and prayers of praise to White and Blue Tara. Owing to her lack of obscuration, pride, and emotionality, she swiftly accomplished great wisdom, compassion, and diligence, while mastering the essential meaning of both sutra and tantra.[23]

She was also skillful in worldly actions. First to rise in the morning, she was the last to sleep at night; she was constantly occupied in farming, the preparation of meals, and the weaving of woolen cloth. In these activities she was expert and her family became prosperous.

By the time she was fifteen, she was well known in central and northeast Tibet. Many young men journeyed to her village to ask for Nangsa in marriage, but she was preoccupied with the pure practice of Dharma and her commitment to care for her aging parents, for she was their only child. Her accomplishments in worldly activities and the Dharma were such that one girl like Nangsa was valued more than a hundred boys. Her parents refused all who proposed marriage, saying they wished her to be their servant in their advancing years.

At an earlier time, in the Gyaltse Rinang Tsochen region, the Lord Drachen had taken as his wife the Lady Sönam Gyalmo. Lord Drachen was sharper in mind than a blazing flame, rougher in manner than river rapids, finer in wit than a yak-tail hair, hotter in temper than an Indian pepper, rounder in shape than a pea. To this couple was born a boy, Dragpa Samdrup, and a girl called Nyimo Netso. Sometime later, the children's mother died, so both the father and his grown son were without wives. His father thought, "For my son I should obtain in marriage the daughter of good family, a beautiful girl."

With this in mind he went to the annual festival of Nenying Zungdrub to receive the lama's blessing and to see the sights, as was the custom of the region. There he saw gathered the white-haired elders and the white-toothed young, male and female, religious and lay people. The Lord Drachenpa[24] traveled to the annual festival of Nenying Zungdrub as a noble with many servants, dressed in rich ornaments and finely clothed, very well outfitted indeed. Thus they went to receive the empowerment.[25]

The girl Nangsa also went early to the festival to receive the blessings, a lovely maiden dressed splendidly. It was her first time in public. Her parents encouraged her to go. They wished her to succeed, to shine in the crowd, her face like the full moon, dressed and adorned beautifully, her hair gleaming like salu grass.[26] Her parents had sent all the necessities along with her, food and so on, carried by her female servant, Dzomkyi. She went before the Buddha

image at Nenying Monastery, making customary offerings to the Buddha, Dharma, and Sangha, then offered a kata [27] to the Lama and requested his blessings. They attended the Nenying Festival, going among the people who were receiving blessings and initiation and making offerings to the Lama. To the objects of devotion they made prostrations, performed circumambulations,[28] and made offerings. Later, they went to see the yearly performance of the lama dance.[29] There they sat among many girls in the large crowd.

The Lord Drachen's family and servants were also present at the performance, watching from the Nenying Lama's upstairs balcony. But the Lord Drachen did not watch the dance; his eyes were on Nangsa, his gaze following wherever she went. Losing his composure, he ordered his steward Sönam Palkye to snatch Nangsa from the crowd like a bird caught by a falcon or a rabbit carried off by an eagle.

When she was brought before him, Lord Drachen seized the hem of Nangsa's long dress with his left hand and passed a full cup of wine to the girl with his right, saying:

"Beautiful body, lovely voice, delicious fragrance, sweet tasting and smooth to the touch, possessor of the five supremely desirable qualities,[30] are you a god, a naga deity princess, an apparition, or a human? Whose daughter are you? Do not be coy, whose child are you? Speak truthfully, what is your father's name, girl? What is your mother's name? What is your name? In what region do you live, what is the name of your homestead? I am the Lord of Nyangtö Rinang, with the name of Drachen, as renowned as the dragon. My heir Dragpa Samdrup is the fortified wall of my treasury and its hidden precious jewel. He has attained the age of manhood, six times three years. Will you be his wife?"

So he spoke.

Disturbed by these words, Nangsa quickly thought, "Although I wish to practice pure Dharma, my real enemy is my beautiful face, for what is offered to me now is just a worldly marriage. What shall I do?" She began to sing this song: "Supreme Mother of the Victorious Ones, Lady Tara, look upon me, this girl without Dharma."

Then she answered Lord Rinangpa:

"Hear me, Lord Drachen, sir. My country is Nyangtö Gyaltse; my birthplace is Jangepekü. My father's name is Kunzang Dechen, my mother is Nyangtsa Saldrön. My name is Nangsa Wöhbum; an ordinary householder's daughter am I. The poisonous rhododendron is beautiful but is not used to adorn an altar. Though the color of a dholo[31] is bright blue, its beauty cannot be compared with that of the turquoise. Though the young sparrow learns to fly, it will never soar as the vulture. My face may be pretty, but how could I ever be lady to a lord of such might? Let me go, please. I will not live in a home, but will instead go practice Dharma."

Thus she spoke.

The Lord's servant, Sönam Palkye, took Lord Drachen's turquoise necklace and tied it with a red silk cord to a ceremonial arrow decorated with five colored silk ribbons. He handed it to Lord Drachen and said, "It is sometimes said,

'When a young man goes off to war, it is an unhappy event with a joyful pretense, but when a girl is engaged to be married, it is a happy event with a sad pretense.' Nangsa really wishes to marry this great lord, but in public she must protest. Instead of this, isn't it better to just place upon her the turquoise and flags fastened to the arrows?"

Again the Lord Drachen decided to speak his mind, for he believed his servant's words were true, and he said: "I am not satisfied merely looking at your pretty face, you of charming body, much like a goddess. I am the Lord Drachen, famous as the dragon, a powerful figure in this world. If you do not listen to the words of a powerful prince, though clever and intelligent, you really are a fool. This girl who wants to practice Dharma will not be allowed to lead a life of prayer. This girl who wishes to stay at home with her parents will not be allowed to stay with them. The sun follows a path high in the sky, while in contrast the lotus grows low. Though there are differences between high and low, those with positive karmic links can help each other through love and affection.

"The vulture-feathered arrow is long, the horn bow which shoots it is short, yet both interact harmoniously. Positive karma provides mutual support in love. The great ocean is huge; tiny the young golden-eyed fish. Though there is a difference in size between large and small, those having a good karmic relationship support each other through love. The Lord Dragpa Samdrup is powerful; Nangsa Wöhbum is a common girl.

Though there are great differences in power and authority, because of their positive karmic connection they should be married."

Holding a five-colored pennanted arrow and a spirit-stone turquoise that wreathed the two with light, Lord Drachenpa placed a crown upon the head of Nangsa, taking her as bride for the Lord Nyangtö Rinang. He said: "Listen, all people and gods gathered here! Today the girl Nangsa Wöhbum has been engaged in marriage to the Dragpa Samdrup of Nyangtö. Therefore from this day forward, the girl Nangsa is not to be seized by men of great power, nor is she to be kidnapped by people of little power. Ordinary men cannot ask the girl's hand in marriage. It will not do to say she has magically flown into the sky. It will not do to say she has fled into the ground. All should be aware that the Lord Rinang totally possesses the girl Nangsa." Saying this, he placed the turquoise headdress and the pennanted arrow upon her head. Then he released her.

When they had the opportunity, Nangsa and her servant Dzomkyi hid the turquoise and the pennanted arrow, and went home to her parents where she continued to serve them as before. There they stayed.

The Lord Drachen and his entourage returned to Rinang where they prepared for the dowry ritual. They wore ornaments and prepared the wine for the bridal negotiations and the dowry settlement. Then Lord Drachenpa and his servant, Sönam Palkye, traveled alone in simple style to Nangsa's home and knocked on the door. Her mother, Nyangsta Saldrön, looked out from the bedroom window and recognized the Lord Drachen of Rinang and his servant. She said to her husband:

"Kunzang Dechen, listen to Nyangtsa Saldrön! The Lord Drachen and his servant have arrived at our door downstairs. Isn't it best to welcome them, entertain them, give them service, and pay them respect?"

The father responded,

"Hear me, Nyangtsa Saldrön, listen to Kunzang Dechen. I see no difference between the Lord Drachen arriving at our door and an owl landing on our roof.[32] I will not be a party to his talk. Tell him I am not here. Turn him away. If in his impertinence he doesn't leave, be sure to ask why he's here."

Nyangtsa Saldrön took a bottle of wine and ceremonial scarf in hand, and went to the door. Lord Drachenpa and his servant explained all that had gone before and, hearing this, the mother went away happily to tell Nangsa's father the news. The father was also very pleased, and he thought that if there

was no hidden motive, it would be excellent for Lord Drachenpa to ask for Nangsa's hand in marriage, for certainly Nangsa would be offered a wonderful home. "Who is greater in this country?" he thought. "Certainly there is none other; it would be wise to accept the proposal."

They invited Lord Drachen of Rinang and his servant to enter their house and offered them liberal hospitality. The Lord and his servant in turn presented the begging wine and the price of nursing the girl,[33] and ornamented Nangsa splendidly. The Lord Drachen said: "Nangsa Wöday Bumpa[34] and the two parents of Nangsa, hear me. From this day and time, the girl Nangsa has been pledged in marriage to the son of the Lord Drachen of Rinang. Therefore it will not do to say that she has flown away into the sky; it will not do to say that she has entered into the ground; it will not do to say that she has been seized by a powerful lord; it will not do to say that she has been kidnapped by thieves; it will not do to say that her parents will not allow her; it will not do to say that Nangsa refuses to marry.

"She is now the Lady of Rinang! Tomorrow is day one, and the day after day two. On the third day, an auspicious time, I will send five hundred horsemen to receive the girl and to escort her. Prepare to send her personal belongings and inheritance. Listen again, Nangsa Wöhbum! When you came to the Nenying festival, you appeared as the shining moon among the stars. In the midst of all the assembled crowds, it was you, beautiful maiden, who caught my eye. Do you not recall the turquoise crown and ribboned arrow I placed upon you? Where are they? Bring them here now."

Thus he spoke.

Nangsa replied,

"This was forced upon me, and I was totally unprepared. I was worried my parents would think I gave myself too readily and they would become angry and rebuke me. Therefore I hid them away."

"If so," said Drachen, "bring them here now." Nangsa went and brought the turquoise jewel and ribboned arrow and put them in the hand of Drachen, and he placed them once again on her head. Then Rinang and his servant set out for their home.

Nangsa knew she did not want to enter into a domestic marriage; she wished instead to practice Dharma, and she expressed her request to her parents:

"Gracious one who bore my body, please listen to me, when I see that

friends are always separated after meeting, I do not wish to marry Dragpa Samdrup. The Three Jewels are beyond gathering and separation; in these I choose to take company. This girl wants to practice Dharma.

"Because everything that is drawn together comes apart, I do not wish to be Dragpa Samdrup's companion. Instead I want to rely on the constant companionship of the Three Jewels, which, once established, never ceases. In the practice of Dharma I will put my trust.

"The certain outcome of the accumulation of possessions is their eventual loss. Observing this, I do not wish to own Lord Rinang's wealth. The Seven Noble Treasures,[35] neither increasing nor decreasing, are more precious than the ebb and flow of earthly wealth. I will depend on these and practice Dharma.

"All houses built eventually decay. Seeing this, I do not wish to join Lord Rinang's household. More appealing is a hermit's stony cave, quiet and undisturbed, a sturdy home. You, my parents, have been gracious in nurturing my body. Please let me go to practice Dharma."

Thus she spoke.

Her two parents replied:

"You, Wöhbum girl, are beautiful as a goddess. O one of beautiful body, Nangsa Wöhbum, hear us! The Lord of Rinang, Dragpa Samdrup, is hotter than coals; he is even stronger than rapids running at a river's banks; on this earth his power is well known. Therefore do not say you will not marry. If you are determined by any means to practice Dharma, then the Lord Rinang will surely kill your parents. If your two parents were murdered, even if you practice Dharma, how could you attain the path of liberation? Girl, you must not say you'll practice Dharma; instead, please go and marry Lord Rinang."

Thus her parents strongly urged her, and at last Nangsa agreed to become the wife of Lord Rinang.

From the house of Rinang came a large escort to receive the girl, and from her two parents came her inheritance of rightful portions. As they presented it, they gave her this advice:

"Nangsa, you are superior to a hundred sons. Wöday Bumpa, please listen to your parents. When you go to marry Rinang, you will bring these gifts with you as your inheritance: first, a miraculous speaking turquoise Tara figure, along with sacred images, texts, and stupas. All will be given to you plus gold, silver, turquoise, coral, pearls,[36] and so on, set before an image of the Noble Lady, Green Tara, all comprising

a priceless dowry for you. There is fine silk, brocade, woolens, all sorts of clothing, these are your inheritance. Stores of barley, wheat, and peas are all part of Nangsa's marriage share. We will send Dzompa Kyi and other servants to accompany you.

"Sent from your mother and father's home, you are entering another's door. As the rooster crows upon the rail at dawn, you also must be the first to rise, as attentive in all things as the female watchdog at the door. For the common good, be broad-minded, and be respectful of the son and father. As you are not well known there, do not rush into new friendships, but be modest and sincere. Because your lifelong marriage has been brought about by karma, offer your husband diligence and respect. Treat all the servants equally and be kind. We will fervently recite prayers that Nangsa may meet with her old parents often."

Thus they advised Nangsa.

The inheritance share was then given without reservation to the emissaries from Rinang, and together all departed for Nyangtö Rinang performing songs and dances. Arriving at Nyangtö Rinang's home, they were received with unimaginable joy.

Seven years after her marriage to Lord Rinang, the Lady Nangsa Wöhbum bore a son unlike that to woman born, a prince, godlike. At the great party given to celebrate his birth he was named Lhawu Dharpo.

The Lady Nangsa had long before renounced the faults of ordinary people, and developed the qualities of a wise person. Exercising these virtues, Nangsa performed all her duties diligently; she was a faithful attendant, respectful and virtuous to Lord Rinangpa and their son. To the domestic attendants, male and female alike, she was lovingly impartial; likewise she was concerned for the tenant farmers who lived on her husband's lands. She was skilled in all activities: farming, weaving, food preparation, housecleaning, and needlework.

Because of all her skillful accomplishments, the Lord Rinang and all his attendants became very fond of her, especially now that she had given birth to a son! Moreover, she was beautiful and delightful in her conduct and expression. For all these reasons, the Drachenpa Lords, both father and son, due to their great love and affection for Nangsa, were inseparable from her even for an hour. She was placed in a position of full trust in the household and given a key to the treasury.

Until this time, Ani[37] Nyimo Netso, the sister of Dragpa Samdrup, had maintained control of the treasury and had been in charge of all accounting

of income and expenses. She now felt threatened, and grew fearful of losing her authority to Nangsa. While it was true at this time that Nangsa held Ani Nyimo in equal respect to both lords, Nyimo's servants began to criticize Ani Nyimo because of Nyimo's inferior behavior, and they began to praise Nangsa. As people say, jealousy soon arises between girls of equal rank.

The sister soon devised a plan whereby, in Nangsa's absence, Ani Nyimo would blame her for certain indiscretions. Soon Ani Nyimo told all kinds of false rumors to any young woman who would listen, thus creating much bad will against Nangsa. The Lords Drachenpa, both father and son, were thrown into dissension against Nangsa because of it, and in the end the keys to the treasury were taken from her, and even the clothing and food of a lady were kept from the girl by Nyimo, who enjoyed them herself while angry words rained upon Nangsa. In the end, only worn clothing and meager food were provided for the girl, and in the shadow of these events she grew weary of worldly activity. At the same time, a pure longing for Dharma grew in her heart, but she could not bring herself to speak of these things to the Lords of Drachen.

Meanwhile she kept to her room with her son, Lhawu Dharpo, cradling the infant in her lap, kissing him while shedding tears. As she nursed the baby, she sang this sorrowful song:

"I take refuge in the Lama and in the precious Three Jewels. O Deity and assembly of dakinis, please bless me! Dharma Protectors, remove my obstacles, and grant this girl's wish that I may attain the fruit of the Dharma path. If I had not borne this child, now I would surely be practicing Dharma; instead, the rope of samsara, the endless cycle of existence, ties me down. Little Lhawu Dharpo, I cannot leave you, but to take you with me only makes an obstacle to Dharma. I wish to practice Dharma, but I wear the familial Drachen turquoise on my head. I cannot return to my parents. If I try to practice worldly business, Ani Nyimo becomes jealous.

"Kye ma, kye hu![38] My mind is very sad! My beautiful body, my beloved son, these and all loved ones are obstacles to Dharma practice. In comparison, Ani Nyimo Netso is my main encouragement to Dharma, so in fact she is a form of guru. If Nangsa devotes herself to the Dharma, a lama will appear. In time, Lhawu Dharpo will become more self-sufficient and I will have no further duties. If in this realm of impermanence, death does not come to Nangsa, I will not stay here, but devote myself to Dharma. Nangsa will not stay here, but practice in mountain solitude."

Having said this, she put the boy on her back, and the two, mother and son, entered the flower garden to ease her grief. The Lord Dragpa Samdrup also arrived at this time. After washing his hair, he placed his noble head in Nangsa's lap to have the lice and nits picked off. Because the autumn months had now arrived, the old flowers had been damaged by the first frost. Few new buds remained to feed the honeybees, and as they buzzed about in the fading autumn sunlight, Nangsa's mind was accordingly affected:

"In this life I have been separated from my two parents whom I sorely miss. In my next life if I need the Dharma, I may not find it either. This thought brings me much suffering. Moreover, I am now married and afflicted by the spiteful mind of Ani Nyimo."

She was greatly saddened by these reflections, and shed tears uncontrollably.

These fell into Dragpa Samdrup's ear, waking him, whereupon he saw that Nangsa was weeping. He said:

"Adorable one, with your ravishingly beautiful body, listen to me just this once. Head and body jewelry you have, a beautiful dress, turquoise, and wealth; your body to your knees is adorned with rare turquoise; you are graced with desire for the spiritual, and in worldly behavior show great wisdom to all. As long as you are Rinang's lady, you have no reason to be sad. What is the reason for these falling tears? Whatever you wish I will provide. Do not hide your thoughts; please speak your mind honestly."

Nangsa thought:

"Until now the royal father and son are unaware of Ani Nyimo's evil thoughts and actions; they would know about them if I revealed the truth. If I should allow a conflict to occur between brother and sister, they will become suspicious of each other and will not settle things by talk. But if I tell him only a little, I might gain time, which would be to my advantage. At best, he may grant my wish that I be allowed to practice Dharma. But if that fails, because the relationship of Rinang to his sister is like tongs holding red-hot iron, if he corrects her she will not punish me and my life will be more pleasant. Therefore, it may help to speak."

Nangsa sang this reply:

"To the Lama, only kindly father to those suffering, I prostrate. To the Holy Mother Tara and the assembly of dakinis, I pray. As our karma has transpired, and we are lifelong companions, Lord Dragpa Samdrup,

please listen to me. When Nangsa stayed with her parents, I had my own place to live. But my beautiful face and charming body arose as my enemy, and the girl without Dharma had to live in someone else's house. When I arrived here, I also came as Lord Rinang's wife, and behaved respectfully to the Lord and to the servants. I made all efforts to be friendly to Ani Nyimo, but in her view I was not respectful, and while I bear no anger toward her, she paid for the wine I offered her with water. My good deeds were returned with criticism. If I do not speak, she says I am witless; if I reply, she says I am proud. If I go outside, she says I am a loose woman; if I stay home, she says I am a wallflower.

"When I remember the favors of Lord Drachen, I resolve to work hard to serve and to attend him; when I look at Dragpa Samdrup's face, I think I shall spend my whole life inseparably in his company; when I look at the face of Lhawu Dharpo, I feel like practicing Dharma, but worldly thoughts consume me. When I look at male and female together, I wish to be Rinang's lady; when I look at Ani Nyimo's face, I feel like quarreling and I think I should dispute her views; but when I see death as the outcome of impermanence, I believe I should practice holy Dharma. Now I cannot practice Dharma to prepare for my next life; I am separated from my loving parents whom I need for this life. In longing for her parents the girl sings this mournful song. I would be delighted if my parents heard this song!"

So she spoke.

From the mouth of Lord Dragpa Samdrup came these words:

"Nangsa, it is natural for you to miss your parents. You have not seen them for a long time, so arrange to visit them soon, and do not sorrow. I am sure the malice you feel from Nyimo Netso is not willful, but if this is true, I will warn her. Now our harvest time approaches. Three days from now is the auspicious day for harvest; then you must go to the fields with all the workers. Be sure to obtain everything necessary for this effort from the hands of Ani Nyetso."

This he said.

Nangsa was put in charge of preparing and serving food and wine to all the workers, and she also supervised the harvest. At that time, from the direction of Tö Dingri, two repas,[39] teacher and disciple, arrived at the harvest site. They met Nangsa and sang this song:

"Father Gurus, to you I prostrate. May I lead all mother beings[40] on the path of liberation. If food, material goods, and clothing are provided, a

connection with the pure Dharma will be given in return.

"You, O Nangsa, have attained this prized human life. Your precious human body is like the vivid colors of the rainbow viewed against the eastern grassy mountain; although beautiful, it is without substance. This is the perfect time to enter into substantial Dharma practice.

"You, Nangsa, have attained this precious human body. Like the cuckoo of the southern forest region whose melody is sweet, it is without substance. Now is the proper time to perform the essential Dharma practice.

"You, Nangsa, have attained this precious human body. But consider the famous sound of the northern turquoise dragon: even if the sound is loud in all directions, it produces no result. Now is the proper time to perform the essential Dharma practice.

"You, Nangsa, have attained this precious human body. But consider the Naga Lady of the Western Ocean: although the ocean is full of wealth, yet there is no substance. Now is the time to perform the essential Dharma practice.

"You, Nangsa, have attained this precious human body. But consider the lovely fresco drawings on the central temple wall: although beautiful and attractive, there is no substance. Now is the time to begin genuine Dharma practice.

"When death, the enemy of impermanence, attacks, even the heroic warrior's strength of mind cannot withstand it, while those of timid mind have no place to retreat. At that time, seductiveness will not benefit the beautiful woman; the rich man's wealth will buy no ransom. The noble lord will hold no authority to command. Those without power will have no place to petition. The fleet-footed runner will not escape. Only one opportunity is given to obtain the precious human body, therefore do not leave this life empty of spiritual substance. Now is the time to perform practice of the Dharma!" Thus they sang.

As the lamas sang, these thoughts rang true in Lady Nangsa's mind and she was moved with great devotion and desire for a religious life. She aspired to make offerings to the lamas, but out of worry for her position, Nangsa told them that Ani Nyimo Netso was responsible for the harvest workers. Unable to make offerings to the Lama and his attendant, she said: "Please ask the lady over there in the maroon dress with the shiny face."

She pointed Ani Nyetso out to them, and the repa lama and his attendant went and begged alms of her. Ani silently put her work aside and said,

"Why do you beggars come to us? Summertime is sweet for beggars; winter is sour. When residing in the upper valleys you do no Dharma practice; when residing in the lower valleys you refuse to work. When alms are forthcoming, you take; what you cannot get, you steal. You always lie and practice cunning tricks. This is how you waste your life, repa lama, living a hollow fraud. I do not welcome the appearance of the likes of you. If you need offerings, then the one to see is she whose body is as splendid as a peacock, whose voice is sweeter than the sparrow, whose mind is brighter than the colors of the rainbow, who is more mighty than the mountain. Our lord Nyangtö Rinangpa's lady, the so-called Nangsa, is that one over there. Ask her! I am only one of her many servants and therefore do not have the authority to give offerings."

The two lamas, teacher and disciple, returned to Nangsa and told her what Ani Nyetso had said. Nangsa found it difficult to accept this, and offered the lamas seven sheaves of grain while asking the repas where they came from and where they were going. She graciously said,

"I, the girl Nangsa, seek your blessing that I might again meet with the Dharma teachings later in life. Please pray for this."

The two repa lamas, master and attendant, responded to Nangsa's request in song:

"Prostrations to the Father! We supplicate that the six sorts of mother sentient beings[41] will be led into the path of liberation. Once again, kindly listen, young Lady Nangsa. We thank you for the gift of alms you have granted. We have come from the direction of Latö, from the hillsides of the Lachi snow mountain of Tö. I am Milarepa's disciple; my name is Rechung Dordrag. This is my assistant repa; he is called Rinchen Dragpa.

"We are now going toward central Tibet, to the principal village, Yarlung Kyorpo. In the upper valleys we will perform meditation practice, and in the lower region a patron[42] is providing food for the two of us. Auspicious interdependence between patron and repas will enable us to obtain enlightenment together. The cause of interdependence is dedication. On the one hand, Nangsa has made a food offering to the repas; on the other, the two repas create for Nangsa the connection with the Dharma teachings. The seed of interdependence is the blessing of the repas, for the pure Dharma is its essence. I will make aspiration that this essence will be realized."

Thus they sang.

Even greater faith grew in Nangsa, and she offered an additional three sheaves of grain, performed prostrations, and requested blessings. The two repas, master and student, were also pleased; they completed the dedication prayers and set forth on their journey. But Ani Nyimo had observed Nangsa's almsgiving, prostrations, and acceptance of blessings from the repa's hands, and she grew very angry. Hoisting up the right and left side of her skirts, she took a stick in her hand and confronted Nangsa.

With her eyes now bulging from her head, she delivered this song:

"Your outer body is beautiful and bright in appearance, but your evil mind feeds on poisonous thoughts. You appear as a peacock but house a demon inside. Listen carefully to me! At the Dingri Langkhor Monastery near Latö lived the enlightened Indian guru, Padampa Sangye. In the snowy mountain range of Tö Lachi, lives the enlightened Tibetan guru, Milarepa. Because Nyangtö Rinang is on the route between these two places, repa lamas travel here unceasingly. Therefore, if alms were given to these beggars as they wish, there would be no food left for a mother and her child. This farm, Nyangtö Rinang's long valley farm, is an excellent producer of barley and beans. If all these sheaves were given to the beggars who pass through, you would also be a beggar and be forced to travel with them."

Thus she spoke, and Nangsa answered with this song:

"I offer prostrations to the Three Precious Jewels, the object of my refuge. Look with compassion on this girl with no religion. Now listen to me, Lady Ani Nyimo. Because I did not know what to give in alms, I sent them to you, Ani, to beg. Then you said to the teacher and student, 'I am only a servant; I make no decisions. She is the mistress, beg alms of her.' So it was your choice to send them to me. If alms were not given, if they had returned empty-handed, beggars would have been carrying gossip in the lower valley as crows carry meat in the highlands.

"Isn't it better for Lord Nyangtö Rinang's name and affairs if they say, 'They practice harmlessness, sharing their harvest with alms; they make offerings to the Buddhas and give gifts to the poor.' The wise use of abundance is a virtue of the wealthy. Like the bee collecting honey, the selfish hoarding of wealth does no benefit. It is unwise to call a repa disciple and spiritual son of the incomparable Milarepa a beggar; service and respect to such a one is much better. Do not call me demon. It's not right to criticize this girl's virtuous almsgiving."

She spoke in this way.

Ani Nyimo's anger increased even further. She said:

"You, the so-called Lady Nangsa, are in reality a destructive demon. You were attracted to the master and disciple, the two of handsome body and sweet voice, and therefore gave them harvest sheaves. How could that be true devotion? You have your son in your lap and his father's name and reputation behind you. Because of this, if I say 'one' to you, you answer 'two.' You are only Nyangtö's wife, but I am a member of his family by birth. Don't you realize that I have managed all the external and internal business of the family? Until now I have tried to communicate my concerns to you in words; unfortunately, you have failed to take me seriously. If you do not understand my words, I must speak with you using my hands."

She threw Nangsa once into the sky, and Nangsa fell to the ground as the sun at sunset, where she lay as flat as a shadow in the early dawn. Leaping on top of her, Ani Nyimo beat Nangsa repeatedly with a stick. Then she pulled seven strands from Nangsa's beautiful salu hair and put them in her pocket. She considered how she could deceive her brother, Lord Dragpa Samdrup. Since he loved Nangsa very much, unless Ani Nyimo could persuade him otherwise, he would chastise Ani Nyimo harshly.

As she was considering how upset he would be, her brother arrived. Thinking quickly, she started sobbing, and as she ran to him, she thrust her hand into her pocket and pulled out Nangsa's hair, pretending it was her own. Then, shaking and crying, she sang this tattletale's song:

"Dear brother Lord Dragpa Samdrup, please listen to me, Nyimo Netso! While you have been away, the required work of the harvest has not been done. Our Lady Nangsa Wöhbum has refused to work at the harvest. She has been doing all sorts of malicious deeds and cannot be trusted. Early this morning, two crafty repas with charming bodies and sweet voices arrived here at Long Valley Farm. Nangsa lost her head over them and gave away most of the harvested sheaves. Shamelessly, she was even preparing to throw herself lustfully upon the repas.

"Seeing this, I was no longer able to constrain myself, so I cautioned her, but she would not listen. After all the harm she did, she still expected gratitude, and when she did not get it, she pulled my hair and cruelly beat me. Brother, do not make a mistaken choice between your wife and your flesh-and-blood sister."

Lord Dragpa Samdrup gave careful thought to the matter. He thought that Lady Nyimo Netso would not have spoken so outrageously without proof.

If she had been brutal with Nangsa, surely she would have said nothing. The so-called Lady Nangsa, he thought, is very beautiful and has given me the gift of a son. My father and I and all our servants have greeted her with joyful smiles and cared for her well until now. She has become spoiled. Children and women are alike, he thought; they must be disciplined from the beginning or they develop bad habits.

Dragpa Samdrup sought out Nangsa. When he found her sitting in a corner of the field, he saw that she was weeping from Ani Nyimo's beating. To this he responded:

"You listen to me, Demon Nangsa Wöhbum, give me your full attention! You have nothing to show for the work you were asked to do, but unasked you helped the repa lamas. Moreover, you physically attacked my younger sister. It was not enough to house the stray dog on our roof; now we have to hear it howling at the moon! Warming the wine bottle in the sun causes the wine to rise higher than its mouth, spilling out. Feeding grain to a donkey guarantees that the horse will be kicked. When the boatman knows the shallow places in the river, he can cross with a hole in his boat. When the beggar learns the nature of dogs, he walks with a club on his shoulder. You miscreant demon, Nangsa, take lessons from these words."

This is what he said.

Nangsa thought,

"It is not enough for him to strike home with the arrow; he must also flaunt his bowmanship." She wanted to seek his understanding and tell him: "My Lord, you have accused me falsely! Ani Nyimo not only beat me herself, it seems that she, twisting the truth, claims that I assaulted her. Even more than before, Ani Nyimo accused me of miscreant deeds that I did not commit! If one is never tested, how is it possible to learn to practice patience?"

She thought:

"The minds of my lord and his father will be moved when they hear the truth as I tell it, for they will not allow lies and deceit to prevail. But how is it possible? There is danger that one may not agree, and a dispute will develop. Besides, even if I explain the situation to the male and female servants, they will simply see it as a rivalry between two women."

She remained silent, lost in her thoughts. Lord Samdrup, observing her silence, thought:

"So she cannot deny it! This proves my sister, Ani Nyimo, is right. Nangsa is guilty and now she is crying. Except for her tears, she does not answer!"

This angered him and, grasping her by the hair, he spun her around. Then he began to kick her many times and struck her with the flat blade of his sword. As a result her hands and feet were badly injured and three of her ribs were broken, causing unbearable pain.

As Nangsa cried out, two servants, Sönam Palkye and Dzomkyi, heard her. They immediately threw themselves to the ground before Lord Dragpa Samdrup and sang this song to intercede:

"Please hear us, O mighty one, listen to your faithful servants! If it is possible that this lady has caused you dismay, then certainly your scolding should have been enough. But since she is your lifelong companion and the mother of your child, how can you beat her shamelessly like this? Nangsa's face once shone like the full moon; now clouds of blood obscure it. Her body was as lithe as young bamboo; now three ribs are snapped in pieces. Please stop your abuse, Lord Rinang! Please stop weeping, Lady Nangsa!"

Thus the two faithful servants spoke. Then they escorted Lord Dragpa and Lady Nangsa to their separate rooms.

At that time at the beautiful monastery called Yalung dwelt the holy lama Shakya Gyaltsen. He was the spiritual son of the Lama Rongtön Lhaga, a learned and accomplished Nyingmapa.[43] He had prophesied the appearance of Marpa the Great Translator[44] to Milarepa. Shakya Gyaltsen was the principal and foremost disciple of Rongton Lhaga, and his practice included new and old tantra[45] and especially Dzogpa Chenpo,[46] the Great Perfection. In a vision he recognized that Lady Nangsa's true nature was that of a dakini, and that she could overcome her obstacles to Dharma practice only if she were to die and then be supported in returning from death. Thereafter, he saw she would become a Dharma practitioner, one with the capacity of immense benefit for others, with increased activity for enlightenment.

To speed the return from death of the Dakini Nangsa and to guide her to the Dharma, he emanated into the charming body and melodious voice of a handsome young man together with a playful monkey, and appeared beneath Dakini Nangsa's window. He freed his monkey to perform playful antics while he sang this song:

"O adorable one, with a body more beautiful than a goddess, I call to

you who are seated on the balcony! Watch the monkey; do not be distracted. Let your ear hear this beggar's song!

"In the eastern direction is the forested land of Kong. There each monkey mother has a baby. The most evolved of these perform dramas by dance and pantomime. The less advanced feed on sweet fruit and delicacies. But a monkey of poor karma falls into the clutches of a beggar who ties a rope around his neck. What suffering! This monkey is forced to learn to perform under great coercion. The root of the fate of the monkey lies in his playfulness.

"In the forested country to the south known as Bheta, to each bird is given a baby chick. Those skillful of wing soar up in the sky; those clumsy ones fall into the treetops. The parrot that speaks may come into the hands of a king, but the ring around his leg causes much hardship. It is very difficult for the parrot to learn the human language. The root of the fate of the parrot is his potential for speech.

"Western Nepal is a country of rice plantations. There each iridescent golden mother bee tends to her baby. Those who are adept at food gathering take much nectar. One less fortunate may circle and alight on the jug of rice wine. This poor bee may fall captive to a child. When pressed in its fingers, what suffering it feels! When the honey gatherers come, bees are expelled from their hives; what a hardship this is! The root of the fate of the bee lies in the sweetness of its honey.

"In the grassy regions of Northern Mongolia, each mother sheep nurtures her lamb. The fat white lambs nibble succulent grass; the scrawny lambs are led by pilgrims in circumambulation of sacred places. The short-lived lambs fall into the hands of the butcher. There they must endure the suffering of slaughter. Because of desire for meat, all kinds of misery arise. The root of the fate of the lambs is the tastiness of their meat.

"In the central golden Nyangtö valley, each young woman is given a girl to mother. Those girls blessed with the karma to enter the spiritual path go into retreat; those less fortunate remain with their parents. The beautiful girl is delivered as bride into the hands of the Lord; what hardships she suffers at the hands of Ani Nyimo! Through envy, much suffering arises. The root of the fate of the girl is her beauty.

"If the heart does not sense the impermanence of death, even if the body is beautiful, it is no more unusual than the display of the Indian peacock. This precious life is worthless if Dharma is not practiced. Having obtained this valuable human body, a melodious voice is no more exceptional than the song of the sparrow in the park. All is for

naught if Dharma is not practiced. If you do not give alms to a beggar like me, though you wear precious ornaments, they are without substance as a painting on a temple wall."

The beggar sang this song as the monkey continued to dance. Nangsa was captivated by the beggar's song, as her son, Lhawu Dharpo, was entranced by the monkey's dance. As mother and son watched, Nangsa thought that she should give alms to the beggar of barley, tsampa,[47] tea, butter, gold, silver, silk, and fine cloth, but she thought,

"I cannot give without asking Ani Nyimo, for I would then arouse her wrath. How can I fulfill the beggar's desire? If I ask Ani Nyimo, I cannot expect other than punishment, and it would be impossible to fulfill the beggar's wishes."

The alternative, she thought, would be to give what she herself already owned, namely heirlooms of clothing and jewelry given to her by her parents. "I might then ask the beggar if, in his travels, he has come across a pleasantly situated monastery whose abbot has excellent spiritual qualities. I must practice Dharma without attachment to my son or parents. If I do not enter Dharma practice now without attachment to my parents and son, then I hope to enter practice before I die after I have raised my son and when my duty to my parents has ended. Only yesterday I heard the song of the two yogi lamas; today I've heard the beggar's song. Both were addressed to me and have to be omens. For that reason I must resolve to enter the Dharma." So she thought.

Inviting the beggar and his monkey into her private quarters, she sang this song:

"Please listen, traveler. Monkey-beggar, listen to this girl, Nangsa. When I last looked upon my parents, I saw old age coming upon them like shades of evening. In their last years I will be unable to serve them. When I think upon this, my mind becomes saddened. I will not stay here; I will go and practice Dharma. Wöday Bumpa will enter solitary retreat.

"When I look at my days, I recall I am married for life, yet others so easily influence my life partner, he wavers like a flag blown by the wind. He can't keep his own mind when he listens to others. I can't defend myself while he is scolding me. When I think upon this, my mind becomes saddened. Nangsa will not stay, but will go and practice Dharma. I, Wöday Bumpa, will enter solitary retreat.

"When I look at this child, Lhawu Dharpo, brought to me by karmic debt,

he appears as a rainbow before a green mountain meadow, beautiful, yet without the least substance. When I think upon this, my mind becomes saddened. Nangsa will not wait, but will enter into Dharma practice. Wöday Bumpa will enter into solitary practice.

"When I look at Ani Nyimo, I see that she is jealous as a snake. Though I practice patience, she provokes much anger in me. When I think upon this, my mind becomes saddened. Nangsa will not wait, but will enter Dharma practice. Wöday Bumpa will enter into solitary practice.

"When I look at the male and female servants, I think of them as children. Their minds contain thoughts, but they cannot express them. When I think upon this, my mind becomes saddened. Nangsa will not wait, but will enter into Dharma practice. Wöday Bumpa will enter solitary hermitage. In order to enter retreat, this girl will find a monastery where it is pleasant to stay and there begin to practice Dharma. Which lama has the greater blessing if approached?"

She spoke:

"You, the beggar who travels freely in all regions, must have useful tales and information from your talks with people. I will give you gifts of jewels and precious coral. Do not hide the truth; please answer all my questions now."

Thus she spoke, and the beggar, kneeling to the ground on one knee respectfully, joined his hands together as in prayer. Then he sang this song:

"You of beautiful body, Nangsa Wöhbum, listen to me. There is no country that I have not seen. I have traveled throughout Ü, Tsang, Dhak, and Kong. All the talk I have heard centers around one clear fact: the Ü and Tsang regions are where the Dharma has developed well, where one mountain solitude is more pleasant than the next for meditation, and where each lama's blessing is greater than the last. And there are many lamas, so it is difficult to choose, but in these times the greatest activity of benefiting beings is to be found in the snow mountain range in Upper Lachi. There the yogi Milarepa abides.

"The distance is great and the road difficult, and you, lady, will not be able to reach it. But near here to the north and easily accessible is the pleasant monastery, Sera Yalung, flanked to the rear by the sky-leaping lion mountain and to the front by the reclining elephant mountain. There the good Lama Shakya Gyaltsen abides, very learned and accomplished, and well known for his knowledge of the pure Dharma teachings of Dzogchen. If the lady wishes to enter into Dharma practice, she should travel there; if Nangsa is looking for an accomplished Lama,

she should meet this one."

Thus he spoke, and Nangsa Wöhbum, at the sound of the name of Lama Shakya Gyaltsen, felt the fine hairs of her body tingle as tears fell from her eyes. From among her jewels Nangsa took five large pieces of coral and three outstanding specimens of turquoise, and she presented them to the beggar.

Just at that time, Lord Drachenpa thought he should go out to the fields to check the progress that the field hands had made in the harvesting, and he left his quarters. He heard the voice of a young man coming from Nangsa's room, their songs echoing back and forth. He thought:

"The voice of the woman is certainly Nangsa's, but that of the male is sweeter than that of my son, Dragpa Samdrup. Who can this be?"

He peeked through a crack in the door to Nangsa's room and saw the baby Lhawu Dragpo playing with the monkey as the beggar sat before Nangsa. He saw that she had loosened the corals and turquoise from her headdress and was presenting them as a gift to the beggar. He remembered that Nangsa had given numerous sheaves of grain to wandering repas a few days earlier, and thought that Nangsa must have become quite scatterbrained. Though his daughter Nyimo had advised Nangsa strongly against such practices, she had failed to listen. Moreover, he had heard that Nangsa had beaten Nyimo in response, and that she had told Dragpa Samdrup. Because of this she had been moderately punished, yet he beheld her entertaining a beggar in her room and lavishly giving him her ornamental coral and turquoise. Such bad manners cast a cloud of ill repute upon Nangsa! He thought,

"How can she be fit to manage the house of a lord like Nyangtö Rinang? Besides, this cannot possibly turn out well for their son, Lhawu Dharpo."

With these conclusions, he decided to confront Nangsa immediately. He burst through the doorway, at which point the beggar and his monkey seemed to jump out the window, but when he went to look for them he could not find them or see where they had gone. Grabbing Nangsa's hair, he spoke thus to her:

"Listen to me, you promiscuous tramp! Listen to me, the Lord Drachen, father of the Rinang Lord. Not only have you extravagantly given sheaves of grain to those two repas, today you gave your personal jewelery to that beggar. It is an even greater misdeed that you invited him into your quarters in the house of the Lord Drachen. This confirms, of course, the

story of Nyimo Netso and also of Dragpa Samdrup. This shows that you are a whore, an evil woman, spoiled and self-serving."

Saying this, and without waiting for Nangsa's reply, he began to beat her, even though the injuries she had received earlier had not yet healed. Then, snatching the child Lhawu, Lord Drachenpa carried him off like a sparrowhawk and left him with a woman servant.

Grieving for the loss of her son, Nangsa became depressed, and later that evening she died of a broken heart alone in her bed. During the night the boy Lhawu Dharpo sensed that his mother had passed away, and because of his grief and the fact that he had been separated from her, he cried endlessly from the onset of night until the coming of morning.

At daybreak, the nurse, without speaking to either of the lords, father or son, decided to return the baby to Nangsa. Outside Nangsa's room she heard no sound within. Since Nangsa usually awoke early, she thought this unusual. When she approached the bed, she saw Nangsa alone, wreathed by her flowing black hair, and thought, "Lady Nangsa is sleeping in her bed." So she said:

"Lady Nangsa! Please do not sleep, wake up!" Hearing no answer, she put her hands beneath the covers and found that Nangsa's body was completely cold. Yet she could not believe it, and checking further, determined that Lady Nangsa lay dead.

She hurried before the Rinang lords to tell them that Nangsa had passed away. Father and son quickly went to Nangsa's room to see for themselves if this were true. Looking upon her, they remembered the sheaves of grain that she had presented to the two repas, and the turquoise and coral she had given to the beggar with the monkey. "We had to punish her for those deeds," they thought, "and now, because of her displeasure, she is pretending to be dead."

The father and son, each seizing one of Nangsa's hands, pulled her up still believing that she was faking, and sang this song:

"Listen to us, beautiful young friend! Listen to the two of us, father and son. High in the sky, the bright shining moon sometimes pretends to be eclipsed by the planet Rahu.[48] However, since the moon is not yet full, it cannot be eclipsed. Girl, do not sleep, you must get up! Nangsa, please do not sleep; wake up. Below, in the garden, the lotus flower is pretending to be damaged by frost, but hailstones may have really damaged it. Since autumn has not yet arrived, how can it be frostbitten?

Girl, do not sleep, you must get up. Nangsa, please do not sleep; wake
up. In a warm bed in a pleasant room, the Lady Nangsa pretends to be
dead. Though in your body there may be pain and suffering, you are
not hurt enough to die."

Saying this, the father and son both pulled Nangsa by the hands up
from the bed.

But of course, Nangsa could not answer. Her body had become cold,
she could not hold herself erect, and her stream of breath had stopped.
All of these signs confirmed Nangsa's death and both father and son grew
remorseful, but they could think of nothing further to do. To fulfill her wishes,
they made offerings to the supreme and precious Buddha, gave gifts to the
poor, and very generously provided for the Sangha.

Then they called in an astrologer who, upon completing his calculations, determined that Nangsa had not come to the end of her natural life,
that she had not completed her karma, had not consumed this lifetime's food
and drink. He advised them to move her body to the top of a mountain in
the east.

"After seven days and nights, you can either throw her body in the
water, or take her away for a vulture sky burial, burn it in fire, or give
it to dogs, whatever you like."

Thus advised by the astrologer, they placed Nangsa's body on a wooden
throne, her body well wrapped in cotton with a white woolen cloth tied over
it. It was then placed on the grassy mountaintop that was shaped like an
elephant extending its trunk to the east of Nyangtö Rinangpa's house. So that
birds, dogs, or other animals would not disturb the body, the porters camped
nearby where they made a fire and boiled tea.

At that time the consciousness of Lady Nangsa, like a hair pulled out
of butter, wandered in the sipa bardo.[49] The messengers of the lord of death,
Awa Lango among them, brought her before the lord, King of Dharma. He is
the judge of those who die: those of good karma go further on the path of
liberation to a higher rebirth, as though a white cloth was laid out for them
to walk upon. They evolve onward, while those who perform negative deeds
descend to the three lower realms[50] and the eighteen regions of hell. This is
where the black path downward leads. Beings in the hot hell suffer severely
on a ground of searing iron or by being boiled in a pot of hot lava. Those in
the cold hell realm are placed between a snowy mountain and the edge of
an icy glacier, thus suffering from extreme cold.

Nangsa witnessed countless unimaginable sufferings in these hells, and was very frightened by it all. Before the Dharma King, the Lord of Death, she knelt, joined her hands together, and prayed:

"Lady Tara, I appeal to you, look graciously upon me. Bless me, O Mother of the Buddhas and assembly of dakinis! King of Dharma, Lord of Death, you who examine one's virtuous and sinful life deeds, listen to this girl. At the time I was alive, before my death, when I was living in the realm of humans, I was physically unable to practice pure Dharma, yet I wished to be helpful to all beings. Understanding that death always follows birth, I have not become attached to my beautiful body. Realizing that all accumulated wealth is eventually lost, I have not been miserly and have given alms and offerings. Recognizing that all friendly gatherings end in separation, I have not become consumed by love for close relatives. I have realized that patience is the heart of Dharma, and so have not become angry with the enemy who hates me. O Lord of Death, Dharma King, you who judges the good and evil actions of the virtuous and sinful, please be gracious to this girl."

Thus she spoke, and the lha spirits, black and white,[51] which were born together with Nangsa, were asked to display the white and black stones they had collected as a result of Nangsa's good and evil actions. When they were piled up there were only a few black stones and many white. Then the Lord of Death looked in his mirror and saw that this Nangsa was not an ordinary woman, but the emanation of a noble dakini, so he said,

"Listen carefully to what I am about to say, Nangsa Wöhbum. Turn your ear to the words of King Yama. I have set apart the white virtues and the black sins that are yours. Those who collect the white virtues progress on the road to liberation. I am known as the Supreme Noble Compassionate One. I am the compassionate emanation of the victorious buddhas of the three times. I also send to hell those who are sinful.[52] For this I am named King Yama, Lord of Death. To those who have created bad karma by breaking their sacred vows of commitment, I am the wrathful lord of warriors, their subjugator. Their overlords cannot protect the guilty; the sinful cannot be led to liberation by their lama.

"There is no escape from this court of justice, but you, girl, are not a sinner; you are in fact a dakini emanation. Just by performing the formal ritual, one cannot gain liberation, but it is certain that by realizing Dharma's true meaning in the mind, one will obtain buddhahood. Of course, practicing pure Dharma both in body and mind is best. You must not stay here; return to the realm of humans where your consciousness

will re-enter your body. Become a Dharma practitioner and perform great beneficial activities for others."

Thus he spoke.

Nangsa was very happy, and prostrating to the Dharma King, Lord Yama, took his blessing. Climbing from the lower realm to the human realm on a path like a soft woolen cloth, she came at last to her own body, at which point her mind entered into it again and she regained consciousness. At that time the body of the Lady Nangsa lay on top of the eastern grassy mountain and was wrapped by white cotton cloths. From her body emanated showers of many-colored flowers, and rainbow colors appeared around her. She crossed her legs in meditation posture and placed her hands in the *mudra*[53] of contemplation. There she meditated on the seven qualities of excellence of Vajrayogini.[54] She remained for some time in the visualization of Vajrayogini and in the samadhi of the dakini in the postmeditation state.

At the conclusion she again joined her hands before her heart and prayed to the five families of dakinis:

"To the trinity of the lama, yidam,[55] and dakini, I offer respect. Please lead those with negative karma away from the cosmic mire that is samsara. The dakini of the eastern Vajra family, whose body is white as a shiny conch shell, in your right hand you hold a golden damaru[56] sounding 'trololo,' in your left a silver bell sounding 'silili.' Surrounded by a hundred thousand peaceful white dakinis, performing pacifying activities, I pray that you decrease all negativity that drains life energy.

"Precious family of dakinis in the south, bright golden bodies you possess. In your right hand a golden damaru sounds 'trololo,' in your left hand a silver bell sounds 'silili.' Surrounded by a hundred thousand dakini attendants of golden hue, O Performer of Increasing Activities, please increase all the positive causes of benefit.

"Lotus dakini of the West, your body as red as polished coral, in your right hand a golden damaru sounds 'trololo,' in your left a silver bell sounds 'silili.' Surrounded by a hundred thousand red dakinis, O Performer of Empowering Activity, empower all aspects of the three universes.[57]

"Karma Dakini of the north, your body as green as polished turquoise, in your right hand a golden damaru sounds 'trololo,' in your right a silver bell sounds 'silili.' Surrounded by a hundred thousand wrathful green dakinis, O Performer of Wrathful Activity, annihilate the obstructing enemy who performs the ten types of evil deeds.

"Enlightened Dakini of the Center, your body as blue as lapis lazuli, in

your right hand a golden damaru sounds 'trololo,' in your left a silver
bell sounds 'silili.' Surrounded by a hundred thousand blue dakinis, O
Performer of All-Inclusive Universal Activity, grant me the ordinary and
supreme siddhis."

Thus she spoke, and those who had carried her body to the mountaintop clearly heard her voice and came near to look. They saw that Nangsa had
used the shroud to clothe her upper body and had made the woolen cloth
into a skirt. She was sitting upright, and they thought that she had become
a zombie. Those with weak hearts fled, but the braver ones picked up rocks
to stone her. From Nangsa's mouth came these words:

"Do not throw your stones! I am Nangsa, returned to life, and I am
not a zombie."

They were amazed, and immediately believed her. After they performed
prostrations and requested her blessings, they left to take the good news to
Nyangtö Rinang and his attendants.

Since the death of his mother, the child Lhawu Dharpo had not eaten.
At night he could only go to sleep after the maid Dzompa Kyi carried him
on her back, pacing back and forth on the roof of the house. Now he asked
her to show him the place on the mountain where his mother's body had
been laid. He said:

"Though we, mother and son, can no longer meet in this life, I pray that
we will meet again in the next life in the Vajrayogini realm."

The maid felt pity, and she spontaneously shed many tears in sympathy
for the boy while pointing to the place on the mountain where his mother's
body had been laid. The young Lhawu Dharpo placed his tiny right hand
above his eyes to shade them as he looked toward the place where his
mother's body had been laid, and he sang this song: "My loving father killed
my mother who was so close to me. The little boy that has been left behind
is like a baby bird cast from the nest to the ground. I sing this sad song in
memory of my mother, because of her kindness to me. If she could hear this,
I would be happy.

"Dzompa Kyi, look over to the mountain where my mother's body has
been laid. The vulture, king of birds, is not flying, nor does the black
raven circle the spot. Instead, I see rainbows and a tent of light. Please
take this little boy to the top of that eastern mountain! Please take me
to the place where my mother's body has been laid!"

Thus he spoke, and by that time the body bearers had returned and

informed Lord Nyangtö Rinang and his attendants of the good news of
Nangsa's resurrection. Then the Lords Drachen, father and son, and the boy
Lhawu Dharpo, carried on the back of Dzompa Kyi, all traveled to the mountaintop to see for themselves what had taken place. There they saw Nangsa
clothed in her shroud surrounded by a canopy of rainbow light while a shower
of flowers fell from the sky. The two Rinang lords, father and son, together
made prostrations to Nangsa's body, speech, and mind, and confessed their
regret for their past hostility and negative actions. They asked that she return
and become again, as in the past, the lady of their household. They made
the following request to Nangsa:

> "We go for refuge to the guru, the only father, and we pray to all the
> assemblies of mother dakinis. Please hear us, Lady Nangsa Wöhbum!
> You of beautiful body fresh as a bamboo shoot, please listen to the
> two of us. We did not realize your form is the body of the deity, of
> appearance and emptiness conjoined. Under the influence of passion
> we indulged in thoughtless actions; we openly repent for the bodily
> harm we caused you. Nangsa's voice in melody resounds as the music
> of devas;[58] we did not recognize it as a mantra, its essence emptiness
> and sound conjoined.

> "Under the influence of anger we used harsh, thoughtless language.
> We both confess we dismissed your earnest speech. We did not real-
> ize Nangsa's mind is a silver mirror in which bliss and emptiness are
> conjoined. Influenced by ignorance, in many ways we dealt with you
> poorly. We both confess to all the grief we caused your mind. We are
> blind and ignorant sentient beings. O noble dakini, Nangsa Wöhbum,
> we rejected your body, speech, and mind, and we confess, regret, and
> ask your pardon; please be compassionate to us.

> "Even if you give no thought to Lord Drachen Rinang, please remember
> your lifelong husband, Dragpa Samdrup, and return home. Even if you
> give no thought to Ani Nyimo Netso, think of Lhawa Dharpo and return
> home. Think of your son, produced of your own flesh. Lady Nangsa,
> please return. Even if you give no thought to the male servant, Sönam
> Palkye, please remember your faithful female servant, Dzompa Kyid, and
> come back. Remembering your long-time friend, known from childhood,
> Lady Nangsa, please return."

Thus they entreated,

> "Even if you ignore your servants, remember the kindness of your parents
> and return home. Please return home, Lady Nangsa."

But the resurrected Nangsa Wöhbum had no desire to return to worldly activities. Feeling revulsion and sadness toward them, she sang this song to the Lords Drachen, father and son:

"To the five families of dakinis who confer the five primordial wisdoms, I offer respect from my heart. Listen carefully, Lord Drachenpa, listen well, Lord Dragpa Samdrup, both Nyangtö Rinang's lords, father and son. Give thought to me, my mother's child, Nangsa Wöhbum, a girl without Dharma, of poor karma.

"Before I died, I stayed in very pleasant quarters, but then, through impermanence, death occurred, and I was taken here to the cemetery of the eastern meadow mountain. Now I feel revulsion toward home and possessions. Toward our spacious house of four corner posts and eight roof beams I feel loathing. My mother's girl, Nangsa Wöhbum, am I.

"Before my death I rode with pleasure upon a well-mannered horse; after death, on foot, I journeyed to the gates of hell. Now I feel revulsion at the thought of riding horses. Even toward the Gyiling horse[59] I feel loathing. My mother's girl, Nangsa Wöhbum, am I.

"Before my death kinsmen and servants hovered around me. After death I wandered alone without attendants. Now I am saddened at the sight of relatives and servants; revulsion arises for kinfolk and friends. My mother's girl, Nangsa Wöhbum, am I.

"Before my death I was often adorned with jewelery and the five fine woolen fabrics. After death, naked, without ornament or clothing, I wandered in the bardo. Now fine clothes and ornaments sadden me; toward gold, pearls, and turquoise, I feel increasing revulsion. My mother's girl, Nangsa Wöhbum, am I.

"Before death I was nourished by delightful food and drink. After death I was not only without food and wealth, I had to leave my body behind. I have no attachment now to my beautiful girl's body. Before my death, my lord protector listened to other people, not to me. My mother's girl, Nangsa Wöhbum, am I.

"After death fell upon me, my husband feigned regret, confessed his error, and begged forgiveness. I feel sadness when I consider my relationship with my worldly husband. Toward Lord Drachen I feel increasing repugnance. This mother's girl, Nangsa Wöhbum, was often punished harshly by her husband when she lived. After my death, he attempted to practice virtuous acts on my behalf. Now I have no interest in companionship; toward Dragpa Samdrup, I feel disgust.

"Before my death, this mother's girl, Nangsa Wöhbum, was the victim of family frictions caused by Ani Nyimo. After my death, hypocritically she shed tears for her misdeeds. Now thoughts of Ani Nyimo sadden me; toward Ani Nyimo I feel distaste. This mother's girl, Nangsa Wöhbum, am I.

"Before my death, I was concerned for my son, Lhawu Dharpo, and worked diligently to care for him. After my death I realized that the child had been the rope that tied me to samsara. Now when I think of Lhawu Dharpo I am saddened. Toward my attachment to my child, I feel revulsion.

"This girl will not stay here, but will begin the practice of Dharma. Nangsa Wöhbum will not stay here; she will go into retreat. Even if this mother's girl, Nangsa Wöhbum, is gone, you will have no trouble finding help. Any beautiful young woman will serve you as a wife; I bid you farewell in the prison of samsara."

Thus she spoke.

The Lords Rinang, father and son, recognized the truth of what they heard and so they did not respond; but they also could not bring themselves to leave, and they stood with folded hands, tears falling silently.

At the same time, the boy Lhawu Dharpo climbed down from the back of Dzompa Kyi and onto the lap of his mother, Nangsa, shedding tears while he made the following request:

"Please listen to this little boy, O noble dakini, mother Nangsa! That you, once dead, are alive again! Is this a dream or is it real? If this is only a dream, then this little boy is very sad. If it is real, of course this boy is happy. It is really wonderful that you are alive after dying! Please tell me if this is true or if you are an ogress who has possessed my mother's body. If you are a zombie, then please kill me now, take my life. If you are alive, please embrace me.

"I, a little boy separated from my mother's kindness, am like a young monk without a teacher. Even if he devotedly performs his practice, how can he hope to attain enlightenment? Think on this and do not forsake me.

"This little boy, separated from his mother, is like a people without a leader. They may pay tax and live by the law, but in reality they are slaves. Think on this and do not forsake me.

"This little boy, separated from his kind mother, is like a young man without bravery or skill. Without these qualities, he cannot aid his

relatives or defeat his enemies. Think on this and do not forsake me.

"This little boy, separated from his mother, is like a frivolous woman who wears expensive clothes and jewels. Despite her fine appearance, she will not find a husband. Think on this and do not forsake me.

"This little boy, separated from his kind mother, is like an untrained swift stallion. Without training, his speed and agility are worthless. Think on this and do not forsake me.

"This little boy, separated from his kind mother, is like the sway-backed little brown mule. Though you give it food and water, it is worthless. Think on this and do not forsake me.

"This little boy, separated from his kind mother, is like a merchant who loses his goods and money in poor trades. Though his mind and body are busy with transactions, his wealth is not increased. Think on this and do not forsake me.

"This little boy, separated from his kind mother, is like a pile of unblessed mani stones[60] piled at the roadside. No one circles these in prayer and devotion. Think on this and do not separate mother from son.

"This sad little boy has been separated from his loving mother. Mother, please, you must return home! This little boy, now separated from his kind mother, is like a bird with a broken wing. When it tries to soar into the sky, it falls to the ground. Think on this and do not forsake me.

"This little boy, separated from his kind mother, is like a barren valley without water or grass. Travelers pass by but do not settle here. Think on this and do not forsake me.

"This little boy, separated from his kind mother, is like a person with severe leprosy. Few come near him, and those who do, feel disgust. Think on this and do not forsake me."

Thus he spoke.

Nangsa felt within herself great pity for the boy, and wept uncontrollably as she listened to his pleas that she return home. She thought, "If I go back to satisfy his wishes, it will jeopardize my practice." She reached down and her hands gently touched his head like white silk katas. Then she sang this song to him:

"Prostrations to the father gurus, respect to the mother dakinis, please listen carefully. Son of my heart, Lhawu Dharpo, listen to your mother's song. How can your mother be a zombie? If I, having died, am resurrected, this is not like dreams and magic, it is real. Truly I am alive. Know this, and be happy! Not all those born are deathless, and those

who died will not return to life. Your mother, seeing this, observes, 'I must practice Dharma right away, because the moment of my death is uncertain.'

"You, the white snow lion with plentiful turquoise mane, do not be attached to me, the white snow mountain. Even greater than I is Mount Everest, whose snows never melt. The sun may melt this snow mountain.

"You, the full-winged skillful white-breasted vulture, do not be dependent on me, this high rocky mountain. Even greater than I is Mount Meru, king of mountains. This rocky mountain may be destroyed by thunder.

"You, the eighteen-point white horn stag, do not be dependent on me, the pleasant upland meadow pasture. Greater than I is the meadow with abundant grass and water. Yet the lush grass in this meadow can be withered by the frost.

"You, the swiftly swimming little golden-eyed fish, do not be attached to me, the upland lake. There is an ocean greater than I. This lake is subject to drying in drought.

"You, the sweet-voiced sparrow, do not be dependant on me, the willow park square. Even greater than I is the forest in the land of nagas. These willow tree leaves are endangered by the changing season.

"You, the silver-winged golden bee, do not be attached to me, the geranium flower. Even greater than I is the lotus garden. This geranium flower is in danger of destruction by hail.

"You, your mother's little boy, Lhawu Dharpo, do not be attached to me, the resurrected Nangsa. Even greater than I are the Lords, father and son. Your mother's life is impermanent; I may die at any time. You have heard what I have to say; Lhawu Dharpo, remember my words."

Thus she spoke, but the boy further implored his mother. Urging repeatedly, he appealed to his mother, Nangsa Wöhbum, in this way:

"O one who always guides with kindness, compassionate mother, hear me! Since my parents did not plant the seed of samsara, how can I be the rope that binds you?

"I am the white snow lion on the upper snow mountain. If I did not depend on you, the white snow mountain, when the harmful snowstorm strikes, how will I live to grow my turquoise mane? Even if there is no snow or rainstorm, still I must remain until I am fully grown. When fully grown, then the mountain and lion can practice Dharma together.

Until then, the sun should not melt the white snow on the mountain. Ask the evening shade to help.

"I am the white vulture high up on the rocky mountain. This high cliff will be a refuge. I am not dependent on you. Even though the skillful archer can do me no harm, yet there is no time for me to fully grow my long wing feathers. Until my long wing feathers are grown, the high rocky mountain must remain. When the white vulture has grown his long wing feathers, then the vulture and rocky promontory can practice Dharma together. Until then, do not let thunder blast the red rocky mount. To help prevent this, call upon powerful yogis.

"I am the little brown fawn high up in the green meadow pasture. Even if I am not dependent upon it, the grassy meadow is very pleasant if no hunters or dogs fall upon me. If the pasture were not his refuge, the little brown deer would not have time to grow his antlers. Until the antlers of the little brown deer have fully grown, please stay with me, O green grassy pasture! When the antlers of the little brown deer are fully grown, then the brown deer and the grassy mountain pasture will practice Dharma together. Until then, do not let the grassy meadow be withered by frost. Call upon the dark southern rain clouds for help.

"I am the mountain lake's little golden-eyed fish. If you do not protect me, pure blue fresh-water lake, even if I am not snared by a wandering fishhook, yet I will not learn to swim swiftly in the deep. Until I, the little golden-eyed fish, have learned to swim swiftly in the deep, please remain, O pure blue lake! When the little golden-eyed fish has learned to dart about swiftly, then the lake and the fish will perform Dharma practice together. Until then, may the lake not be dried by drought. Call upon the queen of Nagas for aid.

"I am the little sparrow in the willow park square. If I do not take shelter in the willow park square, even if the falcon does not carry off the little bird, still there is no time for the young sparrow to learn to sing its sweet melodies. Until then, please provide a refuge for the tiny bird, O willow park! When the little sparrow has learned to sing, the willow park and sparrow can practice Dharma together. Until then, to help the willow tree extend its season, invite summer to stay on as a guest.

"I am the little tiger bee in the flower garden. If I do not depend upon you, the geranium flower, though I may not be harmed by birds of prey, there is no time for the golden bee to grow its silver wings. Please remain, geranium flower, until the little tiger bee can gather honey. When the little golden tiger bee has collected honey, the flower and the bee can

practice Dharma together. Until then, so that the flower is not burned by frost, place an ornamental vase upon it.

"I, Lhawu Dharpo, am my mother's little child. If separated from my mother's kindness, even though I may not be harmed by death, yet I, a little boy, will have no time to fully grow my body. Until Lhawu Dharpo grows old enough to be independent, Mother Nangsa, please stay! When my mother's little boy has become independent, then we both, mother and son, will practice Dharma. Until then, as a protection against my mother's sudden death, please obtain the blessing for long life and perform that practice.

"Although you have been a victim of Ani Nyimo's slander and were beaten when you complained to my father and grandfather, remember that patience is at the heart of Dharma. Do not be angry! Please return home. Your loving friend and kind son makes this request with tears falling. Please, if you do not look upon my appeal with compassion, what kind of Dharma practice is that? Consider how pure your Dharma practice would be! If you remained here in our house, practicing loving-kindness, this would be pure Dharma practice just as it is. Without this kindness what would it signify even if you went into retreat? You would be like any animal hiding in a mountain cave."

Thus the little boy implored his mother.

At that time Nyangtö Rinangpa's servants, male and female, as well as their tenant farmers, made similar requests of Nangsa and upheld the little boy's appeals. Prominent among them was Ani Nyimo Netso, the lady who had done great mischief. Now she confessed her misdeeds with sincere regret. She vowed that in the future, even if it were to cost her life, she would never cause such harm again. This oath she took before Achay Nangsa.

Nangsa took all this to heart. She saw that the Rinang lord and all his people had begged her to return, and that her little boy, though very young, had entreated her with examples from the Dharma. "This is quite amazing," she thought. She also saw that Ani Nyimo had confessed her earlier misdeeds and vowed never to repeat them. This also, she thought, must be the intervention of the Supremely Precious One.[61] If now their minds could turn to Dharma, she thought, this could be a very happy time indeed. So she said she would return for a while in order to fulfill their wishes.

She allowed them to clothe her in fine garments and to adorn her with precious jewelry. Then they all returned to the house of Nyangtö Rinangpa. As they went, a copious rain of flowers fell, and thunder, the voice of the

Dragon, resounded three times followed by many auspicious sounds heard all together. Then the resurrected Nangsa achieved nirmanakaya, the state of luminosity and emptiness inseparable.[62] As speech, sound, and emptiness conjoined, she achieved sambhogakaya. Her mind as bliss and emptiness in union became dharmakaya, and from within that state of clarity she saw the limited insight of Rinangpa's people, especially the Lords Drachenpa, father and son. If she could turn their minds and Ani Nyimo's to Dharma, Nangsa thought, it would be a great achievement.

She taught them the opportunity offered by this precious human life, the death and impermanence of all beings, karmic cause and effect, the defects of samsara, and the benefits of liberation. She taught the principles of the mahayana[63] to all beings according to their capacity. But whatever she taught, the Lords Rinangpa and Ani Nyimo were unable to benefit because of their overpowering mental obscurations and defilements. The Lords Rinangpa and Ani Nyimo were unable to practice by themselves, and could not work for their own improvement.

They were further impeded in their spiritual progress by their suspicions that Nangsa might leave them to practice Dharma. Though they had attended her and offered respect, because of their defilements they were still troubled by their inability to have faith in the Dharma. Nangsa could not practice Dharma either, so she was unhappy and unable to eat or sleep.

Finally, the Lords Rinangpa and Ani Nyimo spoke to her in one voice:

"Listen to us, O beautiful one! We have confessed and repented our previous negative actions; we have made a strong commitment to future beneficial activity. We have done nothing opposed to Nangsa's wishes. Though you have no reason to be unhappy, in the daytime you take no food or drink, and at night you do not sleep. You have no reason to be sad. Are you now suffering from illness?"

This they asked, and Nangsa answered:

"I take refuge in the Lama and in the Three Precious Jewels. Please grant me blessings, Devas and Dakinis. Dharma Protectors, please remove obstacles, let this girl's wish be accomplished according to the Dharma. Please listen to me, father, son, and sister, the three of you! Heed the words of the resurrected Nangsa.

"I am not saddened by not having enough food, clothing, and fame for this life. I have thought about this, and I am not troubled. My body's

four elements have not been disturbed by illness, nor are there other reasons for misery in my mind. Because none of you perform Dharma practice, I also am not free to turn to it. This saddens me.

"Though the house in which we live is like a paradise, I take no joy in this. Though our food is as superb as nectar, it does not satisfy. Though my relatives may be as fair as divine beings, they do not charm me. Though my little boy is like a heavenly child, I feel no attachment to him. I am saddened by the fact that none of you perform Dharma practice, and you will not allow the resurrected Nangsa to go practice either. If you will not let me go to practice Dharma, then let me visit with my parents."

Thus she spoke, and in the minds of the Lords Drachen, father and son, the thought occurred that in the past they had heard Ani Nyimo's slanders, and although Nangsa was without fault she had been beaten, and her tragic death ensued.

"We can understand the ill-will Nangsa may have harbored from the past. These events she seems to have forgiven. Now," they thought, "no one has spoken rudely to Nangsa in sounds amounting even to the buzz of a mischievous bee. When we say nothing, she pretends to be disturbed. This behavior is not right, but care must now be taken that the regrettable events of the past do not arise again. She avoids living a domestic lifestyle and doing any work. Instead, she speaks incessantly about so-called 'essential pure Dharma practice.'"

Besides, they thought that since the day of her marriage to the young Rinang, she had not had the opportunity to return home to visit her parents. This had been delayed frequently as events intervened, and her unfortunate death prevented her going. She may, they thought, truly miss her parents, and they reasoned that if she went to them accompanied by her baby, she would become further attached to them and be unwilling to take up Dharma practice. Besides, the two parents would no doubt advise their daughter to stay with her family and friends in accord with worldly activities. This could influence her, they thought, and they decided to send her along with a good gift for her parents and with the maid, Dzompa Kyi, to carry the child.

And so the resurrected Nangsa, the maid, and the child Lhawu Dharpo set out from the house of the Rinangs toward her home, Jangpekü. When they came to the river Nyang, the waters had risen so they could use neither the Gyaltse nor the Tsechen bridges, and travelers crossed in a ferryboat instead. Then Lady Nangsa sang this song requesting the boatman to bring the boat to her:

"Please boatman, on the other side of the river, row the boat across. As I think about my mother, row the boat across. Remembering Nyangtsa Saldrön, row the little black coracle[64] across. Missing my father, please bring the horsehide coracle across. Remembering my father, Kunzang Dechen, send the boat."

Thus she spoke.

The boatman replied in this way to Nangsa's song:

"There are one hundred people going across the river and one thousand people coming back. There are too many people who want to use the boat; I have no time to send it to you. If you miss your mother, cross the river by yourself. If you yearn for your father, jump in the river and swim across."

Thus he spoke, and Nangsa replied in this way to the boatman:

"Please send the coracle, and do not speak to me this way. Ah chang! You must not speak like that; send the horsehead coracle. What is the use of feeding grain to a horse if you must walk on foot? What is the reason for keeping a horse in the corral if you cannot ride him? Having already cultivated the farm, if one goes out to buy the tsampa, there is not much purpose in planting barley, peas, and wheat. Having committed to perform pure Dharma practice, if enlightenment became an obstacle for oneself, there is no purpose in the yogi remaining in retreat. When there is a boat available on the river, and if one instead must ford, there is no purpose in asking the boatman to cross."

This was her reply.

The boatman answered:

"The wit coming from your tongue is dry; it would not do to wet it in the river. In the mountains bandits have control; at the river's edge the boatman is in charge. If you have miraculous powers, fly over. If you have the strength, build a bridge. But if you are an ordinary traveler, pay the boat fee. I do not bring my boat to people who cannot pay. To shoot an arrow, one must buy the bow. But if one cannot hit the target, there is no need for bow and arrow. To become a rich merchant, trading both in north and south, what is the purpose of all this business if one must borrow money? If a person who wishes to be beautiful is adorned with gold and turquoise, yet they have nowhere to go to be seen, why spend the money? If the ferryman prepares a boat in order to earn a fee, yet does not collect the money, he merely has a thankless job."

Thus he spoke.

Nangsa thought about the mountain bandits' power and about the river

boatman's power, and realized that what he was saying was very true. She thought, "If I do not pay a fee to this boatman, it isn't right." She said to the boatman: "What you said is true. I will, of course, pay the fee.

"In addition to missing my parents, I am also conscious of the certainty of death. Having gone to see my parents one more time, then I will go to practice Dharma. Please bring the boat quickly, boatman.

"The red turquoise from my headpiece I must offer to my lama; the small white turquoise below it I offer to you, boatman. So that I may go to meet my parents once again, please bring the boat quickly.

"My turquoise ring I must offer to the lama; the white conch ring on my right hand I offer to you, boatman. Once having met my parents, I will go to practice Dharma. Please bring the boat quickly.

"My small turquoise and pearl headdress ornament I must offer to the lama; the small Kashmiri amber necklace I offer to you, boatman. Please bring the boat quickly.

"I must see my parents once, then I will enter into Dharma. Boatman, please bring the boat as soon as possible." So she spoke, and then with grace and kindness she removed her jewelry.

The boatman was impressed with her generosity, for he observed that her mind was so compassionate that she offered to give away her ornaments and jewelry without attachment. He was full of faith, and asked, "Miss, what is your name?"

"I am the Lady of Nyangtö Rinangpa, Nangsa Wöhbum," she said.

The news of her resurrection had spread, and when people heard her name, they came from near and far. Those who had faith in her, she benefited greatly. Knowing her fame, the boatman returned all the offerings that Nangsa had given him, performed prostrations, and asked for her blessing.

At that time many people came to hear her speak and to behold her face. They requested she compose a song that would benefit their minds. Taking as example the gift of her clothes and jewelry, Nangsa began this song:

"I prostrate to the Guru, and the Buddha, Dharma, and Sangha. I pray to the deity and dakinis. I ask the Dharma protectors to remove my obstacles. May this young woman's wishes be accomplished according to Dharma.

"Those of you gathered here, male and female, old and young, listen to me closely,"

The resurrected Nangsa sang:

"This girl sings, not to win you with her voice, but to answer your request that I compose a song. Because I feel revulsion for worldly activity, I will compose a song illustrated by my clothes and jewelry.

"This hat upon the crown of my head, what bliss if this were Vajradhara![65]

"Beneath this hat, see these strands of turquoise and coral, what happiness if they were my lineage lamas!

"This crown of red turquoise circled by gold, what joy if it were my root guru!

"This round turquoise which adorns my forehead, if it were the precious Buddha, what delight!

"These 21,000 strands of braided hair, what elation if these were the precious and supreme pure Dharma!

"This red hair ribbon, how wonderful if it were the supreme and precious Sangha!

"This earring in my right ear, how happy I would be if it were the yidam and dakas!

"This earring in my left ear, what bliss if it were the dakinis!

"This crown braid decorated with a thousand pearls, what delight if it were the image of a thousand buddhas!

"This necklace of coral and amber, how happy I would be if it were the protectors of the Dharma!

"This conch shell worn on my right hand, how happy I would be if it were the gathering conch shell monastery trumpet![66]

"This crystal mala that I hold in my left hand, how happy I would be if it were used to recite the six-syllable mantra of Chenrezig!

"These rings worn on each of my fingers, how happy I would be if they were the inseparable union of wisdom and method!

"This spoon hanging at my right side, how happy I would be if it were the bell and cymbals of Dharma practice!

"This metal mirror hanging at my left side, how happy I would be if it were the Dharma offering plate!

"This woolen cloth upon my back, how happy I would be if it were a saffron Dharma robe!

"This blue skirt around my waist, how happy I would be if it were the maroon robe of the monastic!

"This multicolored robe worn on my back, how happy I would be if it

signified leaving temporal activity behind me!

"This apron worn in front, how happy I would be if it represented receiving pure Dharma before me!

"How happy I would be if this resurrected girl named Nangsa would become a Dharma teacher!

"Those of you gathered here, young men and women, how happy I would be if you were attentive disciples listening to the teachings!

"I am saddened by samsara. I will not stay here, but will retire to perform pure Dharma practice."

This she sang in a strong, melodious voice.

All the people gathered there performed prostrations and requested blessings, and Nangsa offered them simple Dharma lessons using as examples her clothes and jewelry. Those assembled promised to avoid negative activities of all kinds and to perform many virtuous deeds. Nangsa felt that perhaps her song had produced some beneficial activity for beings, and happily placing the boy Lhawu Dharpo upon the back of Dzompa Kyi, they set off once more for the house in Jangpekü.

Coming out to meet Nangsa the distance of an arrow's flight, her mother, Nyangtsa Saldrön, and father, Kunzang Dechen, waited with gifts in hand. As she approached, her father held a ceremonial white scarf and her mother held a bottle of wine, for they had not seen her for a long time.

When they met, her parents sang this song:

"O mother's daughter, Lady Nangsa Wöhbum! O mother's daughter, noble dakini! Lhawu Dharpo and the maid Dzompa Kyi, all listen to these old parents.

"Before the white snow mountain is melted by the sun, the returning snow lion relishes its sight. It has been a long time since we met. Has your turquoise mane fully grown?

"Before the red rock mountain is blasted by lightning, the white-breasted vulture in full feather returns with joy to its craggy home. They have been separated a long time. Are your wing feathers fully grown?

"Before the rich green hill pasture is withered by the sun's heat, the brown deer in full white antlers returns to enjoy it. The deer and the pasture have been separated a long time. Are your white antlers fully grown?

"Before the turquoise lake is dried by drought, the golden-eyed fish learns to swim happily in its waters. Are you, the golden-eyed fish, able to swim swiftly?

"Before the willow tree park starts dropping leaves, the melodious-voiced sparrow returns to take pleasure in it. The willow tree park and the bird have been separated for a long time. Are you, the sparrow, still in sweet voice?

"Before the flower in the garden is destroyed by hail, the little golden tiger bee returns to appreciate it. The bee and the flower have been apart a long time. Gold and silver bee, are you in full wing?

"Before death comes to her old parents, we cherish our daughter coming home. The parents have not seen the girl for a long time, and ask: 'Daughter Nangsa, are you in good health?'"

Nangsa replied to her parents as follows: "Listen to me, the resurrected Nangsa. My two kindly parents, who have nurtured my body and mind, listen to me. Following birth, death surely comes to everyone, but returning from the dead is rare for all except myself.

"The harmful rain and snowstorms may threaten the white snow lion with the turquoise mane, but I, the lion, with bravery and skill combined, render them powerless. Thus I meet with joyful mind the ever-white snowy Mount Everest.

"The skillful arm of the brave archer threatens me, the white-breasted vulture with abundant plumage. But I, the vulture, soaring high above, have arrived with cheerful mind at the adamantine crag.

"The hunter and his dogs planning harm assail me, the little brown deer with the full white horns. But I, the deer, employing skilful horn defenses, come with delight to the verdant pasture.

"The baited sharp hook threatens me, the swimming little golden-eyed fish. But I, the little fish, by my swift swimming, stay away from it. I, the golden-eyed fish, have accordingly arrived at the Turquoise Lake.

"The threatening falcon comes near the sweetly singing sparrow, but I, the bird, having learned to disguise my voice, am happy to see the willow park square.

"Birds and garden fowl threaten me, the silver-winged golden honeybee. But I, the bee, nourished by honey, continuing my flight, have happily found the lotus flower!

"I, my mother's girl, Nangsa Wöhbum, experienced impermanence through sudden death, but now that I have been restored to life, meeting you, my parents, is wonderful."

Nangsa told her parents of her marriage to Rinang and her good relations with the people, of the birth of the boy Lhawu Dharpo, of the envious

meddling by Ani Nyimo, of her resultant death, the delivery of her body to the eastern mountaintop, and of her meeting with the Lord of Death who restored her life. Hearing this, her parents were saddened and shed tears, yet they were happy to see her and so, smiling, they took her hand and invited her to join them in her home. Her parents grandly treated Nangsa Wöhbum, her son, and the maid Dzongpa Kyi.

One day Nangsa went into the weaving room and saw the fabric she had left unfinished before she married. She thought to finish it as a kindness to her parents and started to prepare the loom, but her mother said,

"We have many servants; it is a shame for the wife of Nyangtö Rinangpa to do menial work."

Nangsa replied:

"It is only a shame for those who, having the great treasure of this precious human life, fail to practice Dharma and senselessly waste their lives. In your view, it may seem that since I have become the lady of Nyangtö Rinangpa I have a superior social position, but I do not even have the freedom to provide my two loving parents what they need for this life. To prepare for the next life it is necessary to practice Dharma, yet that is another freedom I do not have. Whether one performs Dharmic or worldly activity, each should be completed; therefore allow me to finish this weaving without depending on others."

So she requested.

While Nangsa was weaving, many of the girls her age who knew her and had heard of her fame came to visit. They brought tea and sat around her as she wove, chatting about their beautiful clothing, rich jewelry, loving husbands, and other worldly matters. Nangsa, wishing to turn their minds toward the Dharma by using her loom as an example, sang this song:

"Homage to the Lama, Deity, and Dakini; please look with compassion on these girls without Dharma! Please listen, my friends! Hear resurrected Nangsa. I sing this song to turn you toward the Dharma by example of the loom.

"See as I weave this square hole dug in the earth for my feet, how happy I would be if it were a cozy meditation hut!

"See the small square cushion on which I sit, how happy I would be if it were a meditation cushion!

"I, the resurrected Nangsa Wöhbum, how happy I would be if I could be a Dharma practitioner!

"You, Dzompa Kyi, my maid, bringing me food as I weave, how happy I would be if you, my attendant, brought me food as I sit in meditation!

"See these three pegs on the left and right at the head of the loom, how happy I would be if these were the banners of the victorious teachings!

"This beam of the loom which holds the mesh, how happy I would be if it were the lama's oral transmission of the Dharma!

"This heavy woolen cloth that hangs behind the loom, how happy I would be if samsara were likewise left behind!

"These threads running lengthwise, side by side like mother and son, how happy I would be if they were bliss and emptiness in union!

"The woolen threads running cross-wise between them, how happy I would be if they were the basic nature of the ground![67]

"The tension cord that keeps the weave taut, how happy I would be if this were the ten virtuous disciplines![68]

"This shuttle moving, how happy I would be if it were the source of the prana mudra![69]

"This long, soft, white field of threads, how happy I would be if they were the path of liberation!

"The thread, pulled above, how happy I would be if this were leading to a higher realm!

"The lower thread, pressed down, how happy I would be if it were pressing down the lower realms!

"This comb which separates the threads, how happy I would be if it distinguished between cause and effect!

"This thread guide on the pedals, how happy I would be if it were sending positive qualities and receiving negative![70]

"This stick to clear the tangled threads, how happy I would be if it removed the two defilements![71]

"This fringe at the end of the fully-woven cloth, how happy I would be if it were the full accumulation of merit and wisdom!

"This guide that keeps the cloth width straight, how happy I would be if it equalized the eight worldly dharmas![72]

"The sound of the shuttle striking the loom, how happy I would be if this were the sound of the sacred Dharma teachings!

"The sound of treadles up and down, how happy I would be if they

were exchanging self and others equally!

"The yarn spun from 84,000 strands, how happy I would be if it were the pure Dharma canon of the sutras and tantras![73]

"This fine long white woolen cloth, how happy I would be if it were like this girl's pure motivation!"

Thus she sang, and some of the girls with less mental defilements turned their minds to the Dharma, and began to act virtuously and to abandon negative activities. However, the others, understanding only the lovely weaving references, failed to appreciate the allusions to Dharma and saw instead that she was superbly skilled at weaving. Moreover, they observed that Nangsa herself was young and beautiful, that she was favored by marriage into a powerful family, and that a handsome son was seated on her knee. They envisioned a good husband supporting her and saw she did not lack for food, clothing, or good name. She was well-dressed and adorned with expensive ornaments and turquoise jewelry. "When one is as well off as Nangsa," they thought, "why practice Dharma?"

To remind them of impermanence, Nangsa again spoke to the girls:

"Hear me, my long-time companions, friends from childhood! To obtain this precious free human life is difficult indeed. When at last attained, if one does not practice Dharma, one may fall into the cavernous depths of lower realms. Life is fleeting as lightning in space; it may be present now, yet vanish in an instant. You, my friends, do not wish to practice Dharma, so I will not stay but will enter lone retreat.

"Life is fragile as dew on grass; with the slightest wind, it quickly dries. You, my friends, do not wish to practice Dharma, so I will not stay but will enter lone retreat.

"Life is ephemeral as a rainbow viewed against a mountain meadow; although brilliant in color, it has no substance. You, my friends, do not wish to practice Dharma, so I will not stay but will enter lone retreat.

"Life is fleeting as sheep and goats in the clutches of a butcher; they live now, but die helplessly moments later. You, my friends, do not wish to practice Dharma, so I will not stay but will enter lone retreat.

"Life is fleeting as the rays of sunset; although bright, they quickly fade when the sun sets behind the western mountain. You, my friends, do not wish to practice Dharma, so I will not stay but will enter lone retreat.

"Life is as fleeting as the vulture's flight; it circles for a moment, then quickly flies away. You, my friends, do not wish to practice Dharma, so

I will not stay but will enter lone retreat.

"Life is fleeting as a rodent's refuge in the earth; pulled from its hole, it is snatched away. You, my friends, do not wish to practice Dharma, so I will not stay but will enter lone retreat.

"Life is fleeting as a torrent on a hillside; full of sound and fury, it is quickly gone. You, my friends, do not wish to practice Dharma, so I will not stay but will enter lone retreat.

"Life is uncertain as the food and belongings of a beggar; he may have them in the morning, but by evening they are gone. You, my friends, do not wish to practice Dharma, so I will not stay but will enter lone retreat.

"Life is transitory as an invited guest's visit to a palace; the time spent is delightful, but over in a moment. You, my friends, do not wish to practice Dharma, so I will not stay but will enter lone retreat.

"Life is as fleeting as merchants gathering at a fair; they conduct their affairs, but at the end of the day they part. You, my friends, do not wish to practice Dharma, so I will not stay but will enter lone retreat.

"Life is as unstable as a prayer flag[74] on a small white house; when the wind blows, it cannot withstand it for a moment. You, my friends, do not wish to practice Dharma, so I will not stay but will enter lone retreat.

"Life is fleeting as a young girl's good looks; she is beautiful when young, but when she is old, she is unattractive. You, my friends, do not wish to practice Dharma, so I will not stay but will enter lone retreat.

"The teaching of impermanence is not only practiced by the holy lamas, but should be practiced by all. You, my friends, do not wish to practice Dharma, so I, Nangsa, will not stay but will enter lone retreat."

Thus she spoke.

While they listened, Nangsa's mother, Nyantso Saldrön, came and sang this song to persuade Nangsa not to enter retreat:

"Dearest Nangsa, my own heart, please hear me, your mother! How can you leave your two old parents and go into retreat? Rinangpa is your husband. How can you leave him and go into retreat? How can you leave your little boy, Lhawu Dharpo, and go into retreat? How can you leave your devoted servants and go into retreat? How can you leave your wealth and high position and go into retreat? It is difficult to practice Dharma purely; how can a young girl like you accomplish this? Do not pretend to do what is impossible for you, for you will never practice.

Just practice worldly ways."

Thus she spoke.

Nangsa responded in this way to her mother:

"O kind mother, Nyantso Saldrön, please listen to your daughter, Nangsa. The sun high in the blue sky circles round the four continents; it sets and rises. If the sun did not circle the four continents, Nangsa would remain at home. Just as you see the sun orbit the four continents, recognize that I must practice Dharma.

"The clear, bright moon rising in the east waxes and wanes monthly. If the moon did not do this, Nangsa would remain at home. Recognize that as the moon waxes and wanes, so I, Nangsa, must enter into Dharma.

"The lotus plant in the summer garden blooms abundantly, but in the winter it shrivels up and dries. If the lotus did not bloom or dry, Nangsa would remain at home. Recognize that as the lotus blooms and dries, so I, Nangsa, must enter into Dharma.

"If the clear blue water ran upward in canals, so I, Nangsa, would remain at home. Recognize that as the water flows downhill, so I, Nangsa, must enter into Dharma.

"Even when turned downward, the blazing flame ascends. If the red flame flared downward, Nangsa would remain at home. Recognize that as the red flame ascends, so I, Nangsa, must enter into Dharma practice.

"Each time the wind blows, the prayer flag waves on the mountaintop. If the flag were not responsive to the wind, Nangsa would remain at home. Recognize that as the prayer flag rolls in the breeze, so I, Nangsa, must enter into Dharma.

"To my mother's daughter, Nangsa Wöhbum, death must come at some time after birth. If death could be avoided, Nangsa Wöhbum would remain at home. Recognize that as death always follows birth, so I, Nangsa, must enter into Dharma.

"You, my mother, Nyangtsa Saldrön, are no longer a young girl. If one did not become old, but could remain young forever, I, Nangsa, would remain at home. Recognize that as old age surely follows youth, so I, Nangsa, must enter into Dharma." Thus she spoke.

Her mother thought: "My daughter is now an important man's wife, and does not listen to softly spoken words, so I must order her." She sang this song: "Nangsa, I have lovingly raised you from an infant and

now you do not heed my advice. Are you a karmic enemy[75] transformed into my child? Why should I give you counsel spoken kindly from my heart?

"You are like the vast field of grain in the long fertile valley. Though watered, fertilized and blessed with warmth, at harvest time you have not ripened. If you do not rely on the kindness of the gently falling rain, do not regret it when you are beset by drought and hailstorm.

"You are like the soft fat lamb that balks when the pilgrim would circumambulate the shrine with you. If, in the sheepyard, you also fight your shearing, do not regret it if you fall to frightful slaughter.

"You are like the patient whose four body elements are in disorder. Yet you do not permit diagnosis by examination of your pulse and urine, nor will you take medicine or wholesome food. Do not regret it if you lose this life and go to the next.

"You are the naturally melodious violin with discordant strings. Though the notes are well played, the result is disharmony. Do not regret it when in frustration, the musician converts you into a cauldron spoon.

"Nangsa, you of beautiful body and sweet voice, wife of Lord Rinang, if you do not do as he wishes, and if you do not do as your kind parents ask, do not regret it if your state is neither worldly nor religious.

"If you no longer accept me as your mother, then I need no longer recognize you as my daughter. From now on, our bond is cut. Now go wherever you please!"

As she finished speaking, Nangsa's mother threw dust in her face and struck her with the stick she held in her hand. Nangsa's friends restrained her mother while pleading with Nangsa, but her mother threw her out of the house. Then the mother went inside and bolted the door.

That night Nangsa Wöhbum stayed at the home of one of her young friends, and she thought:

"Because of birth, one must suffer death. This I have done, but now I have been restored to life. Maybe my bad karma is such that I must die again, but I do not know when. At this time I must enter into Dharma practice."

She also recalled the words that Yama, Lord of Death, had said when she was restored to life: "Nangsa, now that you are resurrected, you are to become a Dharma practitioner, for you have the karma and good fortune to greatly benefit many beings." Nangsa thought:

"Thus I have been informed by good authority. So far I have not shown

my mother disrespect. Because my life has been restored, I owe great respect to my mother. I will watch my words, for if people speak too honestly, feelings can be hurt. Besides, karmic debts will create obstacles if I do not act immediately.

"The negative events of my mother's rejection and my karmic attachment to my absent young son can be beneficial if I act immediately and enter into Dharma practice. If I delay longer with my friends and relatives, I will encounter further hindrances to my practice. Since what will follow is unknown, I would prefer to leave immediately for the snowy Lachi mountains in the north where the famous Milarepa practiced, but this is too far for me, one woman, to go. Instead, I will go to pleasant Sera Yalung monastery, and as the beggar with the monkey recommended, there I will seek the good Lama Shakya Gyaltsen. I will go to see him as soon as my hosts fall asleep."

Without awakening the servants inside or disturbing those on guard outside, Nangsa silently passed through Tsechen Gashi and onto the bridge of Tsechen. Just as she arrived, as the full bright face of the moon rose above the eastern mountain peak, she sang this song:

"It is certainly auspicious that the compassionate lama accepts this girl as his disciple to increase beneficial activities as bright as the shining moonlight for all sentient beings." While she spoke, she dipped her hand into the river and tossed water three times in the air as an offering before continuing on her way.

When she arrived at the Sera Yalung monastery, the sun was already rising. As she was proceeding to the Lama's retreat cave, the sound of the conch shell announcing morning prayer met her ears. This made Nangsa very happy, for she thought this quite auspicious.

The Lama had a premonition of her arrival, and he had discerned the lady to be of noble birth and a dakini. He knew that he himself had urged Nangsa to enter into the Dharma, but he pretended not to know of her coming. He called for his disciple Tsultrim Rinchen and instructed him to interview the girl before admitting her.

The attendant went quickly to the door and said:

"Please answer me, beautiful lady. Where did you come from this morning? Where are you going tonight? In what region and place are you staying? Who are your parents and relatives? What is the name of your husband, your worldly companion? What kind of house do you have? Are you wealthy? Do you have many children? Please tell me your name.

What is your reason for coming here? Do not keep anything from me. Tell the truth."

Thus he spoke. Nangsa answered.

"Please hear me, Tsultrim Rinchen, the Lama's attendant! Please listen to me, a girl without Dharma. I've traveled here from northern Nyangtö, I do not know where I'll sleep tonight. I was born in Jangpekü; my father's name is Kunzang Dechen, my mother's name is Nyangtsa Saldrön, and my name is Nangsa Wöhbum. My lifelong companion is my husband, Dragpa Samdrup. My son, born to me because of past karma, is Lhawu Dharpo. I am not poor in food, clothing, or ancestral name. Nor am I deprived of friends or precious ornaments. Yet activity in the world only saddens me, so I have come here, sir, to perform pure practice in the Dharma. Please tell me, O worthy disciple, that I may have an audience with the Lama."

So she spoke.

The disciple Tsultrim Rinchen responded in this way:

"Lady Nangsa, beautiful one with melodious voice, please hear me. You, young lady, and the snow lion are alike in having luxuriant turquoise hair. How can one like you practice Dharma purely? You will not practice Dharma, go back home.

"You, young lady, and the mountain vulture are alike in having a full growth of glossy feathers. How can one like you practice Dharma purely? You will not practice Dharma here, go back home.

"You, young lady, and the deer of the green mountain pasture are alike in having white antlers, richly grown. How can one like you practice Dharma purely? You will not practice Dharma, go back home.

"You, young lady, and the fish of the upland lake are alike in having beautiful golden eyes. How can one like you practice Dharma purely? You will not practice Dharma, go back home.

"You, young lady, and the peacock of the southern forest valley are alike in having a colorful dress of feathers. How can one like you practice Dharma purely? You will not practice Dharma, go back home.

"You, young lady, and the sparrow of the willow grove are alike in possessing a melodious voice. How can one like you practice Dharma purely? You will not practice Dharma, go back home.

"You, young lady, and the garden flower are alike in your beauty. How can one like you practice Dharma purely? You will not practice Dharma, go back home."

Thus the attendant spoke to her, and Nangsa answered: "It is right that the snow lion and I are alike; its turquoise mane came naturally by karma. This is no obstacle to Dharma practice. Please do not speak this way, grant me an audience.

"This girl and the mountain vulture are alike; the bird's feathers came naturally by karma. This is no obstacle to Dharma practice. Please do not speak this way, grant me an audience.

"This girl and the mountain pasture deer are alike; his splendid antlers came naturally by karma. This is no obstacle to Dharma practice. Please do not speak this way, grant me an audience.

"This girl and the highland lake fish are alike; his golden eyes came naturally by karma. This is no obstacle to Dharma practice. Please do not speak this way, grant me an audience.

"This girl and the southern valley peacock are alike; the bird's feathers came naturally by karma. This is no obstacle to Dharma practice. Please do not speak this way, grant me an audience.

"This girl and the sparrow of the willow grove are alike; the bird's voice came naturally by karma. This is no obstacle to Dharma practice. Please do not speak this way, grant me an audience.

"This girl and the garden flower are alike; the flower's beauty came naturally by karma. This is no obstacle to Dharma practice. Please do not speak this way, grant me an audience."

Thus she spoke.

The disciple was impressed to see commitment to Dharma in a person so beautiful in voice and appearance. He believed her and spoke favorably to Lama Shakya Gyaltsen. But the Lama decided to test her further, and he sat upon the hatchway to the second floor and blocked her entry.

Nangsa spoke to him from below:[76]

"Lama who has realized the absolute state of purity, I have come with devotion; my words and my mind are one. Wherever I turn, I am troubled by samsara. Please grant me audience, reverend lama. In this excellent secluded place, Sera Yalung, you are my only refuge. Do not dispose of me like dregs of tea. Please use your compassionate mind to hook me like a fish,"

she supplicated.

The Lama replied:

"The pure practice of Dharma is impossible for an ordinary woman; only an emanation of Tara can accomplish this. Your devotion will not last

forever. Beautiful girl, return home. Even if you cut your braided hair and become a nun, your parents and the Rinangpa lords will place the blame on me. The uninvited guest will be happier if she returns home."

Nangsa answered:

"Tsari Mountain is a place like Sera Yalung. There, as here, are hardships of heat and cold. I can practice and endure hardship. If I cannot stay here, then I will still perform my meditation and yogic practice. I came straight to this retreat place as a fox returns to its den. If even a lame person can travel some distance, then Dharma practice may be done even without food. If you do not accept me, Lama, I will recklessly put a knife into my body."

She took a small knife out of its case and stood ready to stab herself.

The disciple Tsultrim Rinchen, standing next to Nangsa, thwarted her and took the knife away. He shouted up to the Lama: "You must open the door! If you do not give her audience I am afraid she will hurt herself."

Again the Lama spoke from the room above:

"The white she-goat will not follow with the flock of sheep. I want to separate the juice of the brown sugarcane from ordinary tree sap. Know that my questions were asked with affection and earnestness, I did not mean that you should take your life. Your devotion, faith, and desire for the Dharma are especially impressive."

This he said as he opened the ceiling hatch to his room.

He then invited her in and gave her audience. He said,

"You should not be sad. I will give you instruction on the mahayana completion visualization, the meaning of 'Ah.'"[77]

Nangsa entered the room above, made prostrations, and offered her precious head ornaments to the Lama. In turn, she received his blessing. The Lama also recognized the resurrected Nangsa as a noble dakini, a pure vessel for tantric teaching. Furthermore, he foresaw that in her later life she would bring benefit to many beings. Based on the Vajrayogini mandala, he initiated her in the profound mandala of body, speech, and mind. He gave her instruction on oral transmission of tantra and allowed her to meditate in a nearby cave.

Within three months she reported to the lama that she had achieved a very profound experience of accomplishment. In turn, the Lama removed her obstacles to practice and furthered her instruction. Thereafter Nangsa lived very happily in practice under the Lama's tutelage.

At that time Nangsa's two elderly parents and her son Lhawu Dharpo

came to visit her at the home of the friend she had visited. The friend told them she did not know where Nangsa had gone. Nangsa's parents guessed that she had returned to her husband's home in Nyangtö Rinang, but when they arrived they discovered she was not there either. The Drachen Lords started a search and received word that she had gone to Sera Yalung to sit next to the good Lama Shakya Gyaltsen, and that she was staying there performing Dharma practice.

When the Lords Drachen, father and son, heard this, they assembled a troop of armed men aged eighteen to sixty to destroy the monastery, bring Nangsa home, and kill Lama Shakya Gyaltsen because they believed he had kidnapped Nangsa.

As the practitioners at the monastery, men and women, observed the approach of the Drachen troops, they cried out as in one voice:

"By welcoming this troublemaking woman we ourselves will be destroyed!"

They then hurried to hide the shrine images and sacred texts in nearby mountains so they would not be destroyed.

Soon the monastery was surrounded by troops who whistled and shouted and chanted "Ki!," creating a thunderous din while they held aloft their arrows, swords, and spears. The smoke and the dust raised by their horses' hooves obscured the sun, spreading a gloomy haze. Young monks and nuns were killed and wounded in the attack, while others scattered in flight in all directions like a pile of beans struck by a stick.

But Tsultrim Rinchen, attendant to Lama Shakya Gyaltsen, could not abandon his teacher. He stayed behind with his aged guru, who could only walk slowly. To speed their flight, Tsultrim Rinchen tried to carry the Lama away on his back, but the monastery was surrounded and they could find no way to avoid capture. The old Lama was soon taken and, bound with rope, he was brought before the Drachen Lords.

While this was happening, Nangsa was sitting in a nearby cave absorbed in meditation. From that state she observed the illusory nature of appearances and so came to observe the events taking place outside. Finding this unbearable, she quickly rose from her seat and came out of her cave, her worn meditation robe thrown over her robe of white cotton. Running up to them, she seized in her right hand the halter of Lord Drachen's horse and in her left she grasped that of Lord Dragpa's. She cried out:

"Hear this girl, Nangsa!

"Do not torment, you storms of rain and snow! You, storms of rain and snow, will not torment the white snow lion roaming on the snowcapped mountain.

"Do not torment, brave archer's arrow! You, the brave hunter's arrow, will not torment the white-breasted vulture flying high in the sky.

"Do not torment, shepherd's mastiff! The little brown deer grazing on pasture grass will not be tormented by you, the shepherd's mastiff.

"Do not torment, sharp-barbed hook! You, the sharp-barbed hook, will not torment the small golden-eyed fish coursing through the lake.

"Do not torment, large swift hawk! You, the large swift hawk, will not torment the sweet-voiced sparrow.

"Do not torment, planet Rahula! You, the planet Rahula, will not torment the sun, which circles the four continents.

"The Lama Shakya Gyaltsen, lineage holder of the sacred Dharma teachings, will not be tormented by Lord Dragpa Samdrup. Lord Dragpa Samdrup will not torment the girl Nangsa, practitioner of Dharma. The monks and nuns in retreat practice will not be tormented by the troops gathered here."

Thus she spoke.

The Lords Rinangpa looked upon Nangsa from the backs of their horses. They beheld a very plain woman, without ornament, elaborate dress, or jewelry, clad only in the white cotton meditation robe and belt of a yogini. Because what they saw enraged them, they had the aged lama Shakya Gyaltsen brought before them. With round angry eyes they spoke, pointing their fingers at him: "Listen to us, Lama Shakya Gyaltsen, and also all you monks and nuns of this place of retreat! Turn your ears to the Rinangpas, father and son.

"You old wretched dog, behaving indecently with our white snow mountain lioness, have performed a disgraceful deed. What have you accomplished by cutting her magnificent turquoise mane?

"You old rooster, behaving indecently with our heavenly grouse, have performed a disgraceful deed. What have you accomplished by robbing the mountain bird of her beautiful wing feathers?

"You old donkey, behaving indecently with our beautiful wild mule, have performed a disgraceful deed. What have you accomplished by cutting her beautiful mane and long flowing tail?

"You old bull, behaving indecently with our young wild she-yak, have performed a disgraceful deed. What have you accomplished by cutting her thick coat?

"You old cat, behaving indecently with our young tigress, have performed a disgraceful deed. What have you accomplished by robbing the fur of the jungle tigress?

"You, old Shakya Gyaltsen, have performed an indecent deed. What have you accomplished by robbing our Lady Nangsa's beautiful headdress, jewelry, and clothing?

"Though in the sky there are many stars, which of these can compete with the sublime radiance of the sun and the moon? It is too late to repent; when the sun rises, the stars are no longer seen.

"On the earth below there are many princes, but who can rival the two lords Nyangtö, father and son? Now that your monastery has been seized and you have been captured, it is too late to feel regret."

Lord Drachen drew his bow string tight to shoot the lama with an arrow while Lord Dragpa Samdrup raised a sword to strike him. Instantly the lama manifested his miraculous powers, moving the western mountain to the east and the eastern mountain to the west. The wounded monks and nuns were healed, the dead revived, and the lama himself flew up into the sky beyond the reach of their arrows, spears, and swords.

There he sat cross-legged in the yogic posture as he sang this song:

"Though in human form, you possess the minds of animals. Listen to the Lama, you sinful men! There is only one who can challenge the sun and moon, and that is the planet Rahula, for Rahula can eclipse the sun and moon. Father and son, who cannot fly in the sky, you two are inferior and so I have taken Nangsa from you. Listen carefully and I will explain why I have taken Nangsa away.

"The lotus flower is best placed in a vase on the shrine. It is wasteful to leave it growing in the mud.

"The remarkable Gyiling horse is exceptional at both pacing and trotting. It should be raced on a smooth and open field, otherwise there is no reason to give it feed and water, for its life is worn out growing old in a corral.

"The perfectly straight arrow adorned with vulture feathers is wasted if not shot true to the target. Otherwise there is no need to strain the bow with string. The arrow is wasted when left to age unused in the quiver.

"There is no use in trying to catch the beautiful goddess of the heavenly realm with a lasso if she does not wish to become King Norsang's

queen. It is a shame for her to grow old, caught by the hands of a lower-caste hunter.

"Just so, if you do not let the nobly-born Nangsa practice Dharma, then she cannot benefit from having attained this precious human life. It would be appalling for her to grow old in the house of a sinful lord. Thinking on this, I placed her into Dharma practice. I, who know how to shoot the straight arrow, have drawn it in the strung bow.

"One who is pretty should dress well and wear jewelry. Having wealth, one should make loans to others. Having studied to be a doctor, one carries the physician's medical bag. Having learned to practice Dharma, I can demonstrate my accomplishment. Even if one has foresight and miraculous power, if the circumstances are untimely, it is wrong to practice and the powers are best kept secret. At this time I am performing miracles to bring into the Dharma those people who possess the ten negative qualities and are enemies of Dharma. Nangsa, it is now time for you to show the miraculous results of your practice and thereby raise the faith and devotion of sinful people."

Thus he spoke.

Immediately the white cotton robes of Nangsa spread like wings and she flew into the sky, soaring like a vulture and flying swiftly like a hawk. As she flew she sang this song:

"Lords Dragpa, father and son; troops and people of Nyangtö Ringnang, all gathered here, listen to this girl, Nangsa!

"You expect me, the white snow mountain lioness, to be restrained by a rope around my neck like a watchdog at some household door. Instead, I will display my turquoise mane high upon the snowy mountain!

"You expect me, the growing young wild mountain yak, to become a barnyard cow. Even if you put a ring into her nose, she would not remain. Instead, I will display my horns upon the wild mountains!

"You expect me, the wild young mule of the green grasslands, to become a pack animal. Even if she were burdened with a saddle, she would not remain. Instead, I will display my courage in the deserted northern wilderness!

"You expect me, the celestial alpine meadow gongmo bird, to become a barnyard fowl. How would I announce the rise of dawn? My sweet voice will ring between the rocky and the grassy mountain!

"I am like the five-colored rainbow, a beautiful display. How could such beauty be contained in the palm of one's hand? Instead, I will display

the magic show of appearance and emptiness in union!

"You expect me, the fresh cloud in the sky, to become a warm soft cloth. How can one wear such a cloud as clothing? I will bring a rising storm with lightning and the thunderous sound of the dragon!

"You expect me, the monkey in the jungle, to become a human servant. What would one expect if a monkey were asked to do the work of humans? The monkey would rather show off his skill flying through treetops!

"You expect me, the resurrected Nangsa Wöhbum, to become the life-long companion of a lord. I would not stay, even if you put a turquoise crown on my head. I would rather display my miraculous qualities by flying into the sky. In proof, I have just now circled Tsari Mountain and bring a gift of its bamboo wood!

"To prove the dzo has walked through the field, he has left a plowed furrow in the field. If I were to soar like a vulture, I would soar in this way; if I were to fly swiftly like the hawk, I would fly like this. In former times, only Lord Milarepa, great yogi, could fly in the sky. In these times, only I, Nangsa, am capable of flying. In the future, only the rare person in Tibet will fly in the air. You, Lord Rinang and your army, do not cultivate negative karma by practicing immense iniquity. It is better to repent with devoted mind to my lama, Shakya Gyaltsen."

Thus she sang, and led by the Lords Drachenpa, father and son, the troops and the male and female retreatants, awed by the lama's miraculous display and the accomplishments of Achay Nangsa, without hesitation understood and made offerings. Nangsa displayed her miraculous abilities to all present. Seeing this, the troops made offerings to Nangsa of their swords, arrows, and spears. Then, toppling like stone walls, they made prostrations to Nangsa and the lama, and sang a song of repentance.

Finally, the Rinang Lords and their troops addressed Nangsa and the Holy Lama Shakya Gyaltsen as follows:

"Regretfully, we confess the following; please listen without anger. Lama, due to the obscurations of our deluded minds, we thought you were a Dharma charlatan, but you are truly an emanation of Chakrasamvara.[78] Nangsa, you are unquestionably Vajrayogini. However, because of our ignorance we were deluded. Without exception we confess and regret our great transgressions. We have accumulated immeasurable negative karma by destroying the monastery and killing monks and nuns. We regret especially the harm we may have committed against the lama

father and mother Nangsa's body.

"For all of these negative acts, we confess with great remorse. Please forgive us, accept us, and keep us in your mind. Our sins are more abundant than a rich man's wealth; our virtuous actions are fewer than a beggar's scrap. Our many lives have been spent without purpose. Please look upon us with kindness, Lama, and do not allow us to fall into the lower realms. We also deeply regret the unvirtuous acts committed in the past and we will avoid these actions in the future. Even if our life is threatened we will still keep our promise. Please permit the flow of Dharma nectar which is beneficial to the mind and easy to practice."

This they earnestly supplicated.

The Lama and Nangsa were very pleased that so many were eager to enter into practice, and they replied in this way:

"Even someone, who through negative actions, is headed on a downward path, may turn around if hereafter he faithfully performs virtuous activities. As the bright rays of the sun are unloosed at break of dawn, the ten unvirtuous actions[79] and the five immeasurable negative deeds[80] will be purified if one confesses them and maintains the four powers.[81] This is wonderful! E ma ho![82]

"If, in the future, one takes seriously the abandonment of negativity and accepts the practice of virtuous ways, this is the way to easily practice Dharma. Listen to this Dharma teaching which is easy to undertake and practice. At the beginning of Dharma practice this is how one should proceed. The lama is the base of knowledge, like the earth. This precious human body is like the rare *udumbara* flower.[83] Its benefit is as great as the wish-fulfilling jewel,[84] of great value but difficult to obtain. Because of impermanence, death appears like a lightning bolt in the sky. Like the fragile flame of a lamp in the wind, the time of our death is uncertain. The possible causes of death are as numerous as the stars in the night. That which supports life is as rare as a star seen in daylight. The wheel of life and death is like the sun and moon's rising and setting. When death occurs, consciousness leaves the body as a hair pulled from butter; the lifeless body becomes inert as earth or stone.

"Accumulated wealth is like the honey in a beehive, eventually used up by others; friends and relatives gather like visitors at a fairground, only to part at the end of the day; friends vanish like wood consumed in a fire; loved ones are abandoned as one crosses a bridge on a river; black and white deeds of virtue and vice follow one's body like a shadow; the eighteen hell realms are the courtyard of the lord of death; the

realm of hungry ghosts[85] is as crowded as the poorest slum; animals are entrapped in their consciousness as a mute man in his dream; the jealous gods[86] are as angry as a vicious snake; even the attainment of the life of a god is like wearing borrowed jewelry. Human life is like a city of shadow beings that dissolve in a moment; the six kinds of sentient beings are full of self-bought suffering. Only the liberation of Nirvana is self-sustaining.

"Compared to a Buddha, the shravaka and pratyeka arhats[87] are like small-minded people, but bodhisattvas are powerful, brave warriors. Practicing the paramitas of the sutrayana is the seed, and the diamond-like stage of tantrayana is the fruition.[88] If one aspires to buddhahood in one lifetime, first depend upon the spiritual friend, with proper motivation and appropriate practice combined. This is the basis of the path. This priceless aim is free, yet hard to achieve. The conditions of freedom and spiritual wealth are very difficult to obtain, once realized, its significance is profound.

"Therefore, contemplate impermanence and the uncertainty of the time of one's death; understand negative deeds; seek positive activities and avoid the negative. One should comply properly by seeking the fruit of positive karma and abandoning the fruit of the negative, distinguishing between black and white deeds.

"One should be detached from samsara by considering its general and specific faults. While remembering the benefits of liberation, enter the superior path adorned with the three practices of meditation on wisdom, discipline, and samadhi. Abandon even the lower path of shravakas and pratyekas; perform the practice in the way of the victorious sons of the Buddha; practice the six paramitas[89] and the four gatherings,[90] vow with courage to work to take all sentient beings to the other shore.[91] One must obtain complete enlightenment in order to lead all beings on the path of liberation. Because of the extreme suffering of sentient beings, it is important to achieve complete enlightenment quickly to be able to guide others to enlightenment.

"Therefore, obtain buddhahood without delay! This method is superior to the way of the sutras, and even that of kriya tantra, upa tantra, and yoga tantra.[92] In these other practices, it is impossible to obtain enlightenment in one lifetime, therefore one must enter the profound path of the supreme vajrayana,[93] one must keep the samaya[94] vows and have one's nature ripened by the four empowerments.[95] Through the practice of generation and fulfillment and by visualization, the

two stages will be successfully completed; one must obtain the four bodies of the union of emptiness and skillful means, dharmakaya, sambhogakaya, and nirmanakaya, and the union of all kayas."

Thus she spoke.

Those who were most defiled, even those who behaved viciously, promised to progressively abandon all of their negative ways. The Lords Drachen, father and son, and those who were with them then witnessed the transformation of the Lama Shakya Gyaltsen into the deity Chakrasamvara and Nangsa into Vajrayogini. They appeared as real as flesh and blood.

Then the Drachen Lords made a solemn vow that each would enter solitary Dharma practice. Nangsa's husband promised to give their son his ancestral property when he reached the age of fifteen and then enter into retreat. The elder Drachen, having given all his properties to his son, would enter first. The younger lord promised to follow after his father in his later years. This they promised before the holy lama, the male and female practitioners, and Nangsa. With sincerity they prayed that if they did not break their samaya, untimely death would not come to them. They offered to die rather than forsake their commitment.

The Drachen Lord and many of his followers entered into solitary retreat where the holy lama and Nangsa were performing their sacred practices. Besides flying in the sky, Nangsa left the print of her head and her foot in the rock as though in molded butter where they can be seen to this day.

Lord Dragpa Samdrup and his entourage returned home to complete the enthronement of his son. Lord Dragpa Samdrup, his sister Ani Nyimo Netso, and Nangsa's parents journeyed to Sera Yarlung Monastery where they remained with their teachers performing Dharma practice.

Afterward the young king governed well, employing as his models the ten virtuous spiritual activities[96] and the sixteen stainless rules of conduct.[97] He provided patronage for the spiritual activities of the holy lama and Nangsa as well as the Lords Drachen and the parents of Nangsa, all the practitioners and monks and nuns. There they remained, enjoying happiness and the richness of Dharma. In that way they accomplished the limitless experience of both temporal and ultimate benefit.

# Drimay Kunden

## Narrator's Prologue

Herein is presented the pearl garland biography of the Dharma King Drimay Kunden, The Stainless Omnipotent One.

### THE INVOCATION: *Om Mani Peme Hum Hri!*
Homage to the Embodiment of Compassion, the powerful Noble Chenrezig!

## Narration

In a time that occurred countless eons ago in the great city of the ancient kingdom of Bheta,[1] lived a king named Sakyong Drakpepal.[2] This mighty king ruled over sixty feudal kingdoms and three thousand ministers, and he possessed inconceivable wealth, which contained enough variety to satisfy anyone. Included in his treasury was an extraordinary jewel,[3] the fabled cintamani, that gem beyond all gems that instantly satisfies all one's needs: the precious wish-fulfilling jewel!

Greater than his treasury of precious objects, this powerful king enjoyed

five hundred queens of noble birth, five hundred queens endowed with great wealth, and five hundred queens of celestial beauty. But among these one thousand five hundred queens not one had borne a single son and the childless king suffered very much. To remedy this he commanded the performance of divinations and astrological calculations. He was instructed to make offerings to the Three Jewels, provide food offerings for the eight classes of obstructing demons and to the gods, and to give charity to those in need. If this were done, he was assured, then a son, the incarnation of a bodhisattva, would be born to him.

Overjoyed by this news, the king took pleasure in making offerings to the Three Jewels, providing feasts for the eight classes of demons, and giving alms to the needy. Not long afterward the queen Gayden Zangmo, a wise and kindly woman who was without faults, had an auspicious dream in which she bore a son.

Approaching the king, she said:

"O great and powerful king, listen to me! Last night as I lay sleeping, I had a dream, a happy dream. Out of the 360 channels of my body[4] I dreamed that a blissful wheel[5] rose from my crown chakra. Out of this, a flaming golden vajra[6] emerged, surrounded by multicolored flames, its point extending into space. Rising from that vajra, covered by a canopy surrounded by rainbow lights, multicolored rays blazed in all directions. I was enclosed by a canopy of radiant rainbow colors and heard a white conch horn sound, filling the universe.

"I feel this is an auspicious dream, and from it I take certain omens. In the sacred pure palace of my womb shall be conceived a noble son. In the time of the auspicious conjunction of the planets and constellations, a healthy baby boy will be born. These are the omens. Let prayers for this intention be offered everywhere!"

Thus spoke the queen.

The king was filled with delight in hearing these words, and he replied:

"Agreeable one, Gayden Zangmo, inseparable from the essence of my being, we shall live together always, never apart. If your body is, as I believe, the mandala of the pure essence of the deity, the golden flaming vajra that appeared above the blissful aperture in the crown of your head is a sign that an emanation of the Buddha will arrive. The canopy of rainbow light which enveloped you foretells the emanation of a Buddha. The sounding of the conch through myriad space displays the banner

of spiritual devotion that will be heard throughout the ten directions.[7] Through blessings from the offerings made to the supremely precious ones and the fruit from charitable deeds, a sign from the unfailing Object of Refuge foretells that you will bear a son. I will ensure that precious offerings will be made to celestial beings, and on earth alms in great abundance will be given to the poor. This done, a son will come to the king who is without a child."

Then glorious lamas of the highest sort, endowed with wisdom, rank, and virtue, and five hundred great pundits were summoned to read the sutras and recite mantras. Without ceasing, in every direction and at every juncture seamlessly bound by mudra, five hundred secluded yogis carrying purbas[8] threw tormas[9] and effigies at obstructing beings while reciting wrathful mantras. These pounded to dust enemy vow breakers, called forth auspicious circumstances, and rained down blessings. So the beneficial practices were performed.

All this was done and after nine months and ten days at last a royal prince was born. His first words were: "OM MANI PEME HUM." He spoke no other words but these, and having spoken the mantra of Chenrezig, he wept, for he embodied loving-kindness for all beings in their sufferings as does a mother for her only son. The king and all his ministers were well impressed by this, and they named him Prince Drimay Kunden,[10] for the name agreed with him. Then offerings beyond measure and price were made to this prince, and he lived with his mother and father in the palace called Delightful Abode on the island of Aspiration and Joy, a place as beautiful as if it had been built of precious jewels.

The prince grew rapidly in wisdom, and when he was five he already knew the five sciences,[11] the art of language, and the calculations of astrology. He had also become learned in all the sutra commentaries. The prince then affirmed:

"All beings at one time in countless lives have been our father and mother."

And feeling compassion for their miserable state, he said:

"Kye ma! In the vast ocean depth that is the unremitting cycle of recurrent existence, like myself all sentient beings experience intense anguish. I have compassion for those trapped by the allure of magical wealth and mirage-like possessions. Kye ma! What suffering there is in the three states of cyclic existence![12] Kye-hu! Alas! What can be done to help? I pity the spirit that must cling to the ego inhabiting the body,

a city aflame with the heat of desire. No place to escape!

"I feel pity for those who labor in the fire pit of samsara, for whatever the effort it is always unfinished, there is always more work—what misery! I feel pity for the married couple deluded by the hope of life together forever, also for those whose attachment to their fatherland commits them to stay in a nomadic encampment. All this manifests greed and attachment. Let there be peace for all those in the six realms of existence. All these beings have been our parents, yet in the distinction between oneself and another, ill feelings are found. Avarice seeks wealth, but like bees hoarding honey, eventually another uses the goods. I pity all this.

"I feel pity for those who, weighed by their unvirtuous acts, sink into the gulf of hell's abyss and also for those whose ignorance prevents the well-taught truth from entering their minds. I pity myself whose name is Immaculate and wanders alone among beings astray. Yet I, Drimay Kunden, endlessly striving for the welfare of beings, firmly maintain compassion for the confused human crowd. Even my father's massed wealth is held back as a resource not put to good use. Should I not draw on these riches to practice generosity?"

This he asked.

The father replied:

"My own Drimay Kunden, the living essence of your name! I suffered unimaginably before you came to me. Now you are free to dispense as you please my wealth and long-hoarded treasures."

That was his declaration. Then did the prince dispense alms without measure, and the suffering of the needy was lessened in the kingdom.

At that time the evil minister, Taradzay, came before the king and made this entreaty:

"Alas, great king who holds power over men, please hear me! All the treasures you have accumulated have been scattered by Drimay Kunden. Now that you are an impoverished king, you will be subject to the rule of others. Do not let this happen. Marry the prince to a fair young noblewoman. Let him become used to comfort and wealth."

This was his plan.

Thereupon all the king's ministers held counsel and chose for the prince Menday Zangmo, the beautiful daughter of King Dawa Zangpo of the country known as Pema Chen.[13] This adorable princess had all the qualities of a goddess: her face filled with light, she was fragrant, devoted, interested

in spirituality, tolerant, generous, and adorned with precious jewels. She was brought as a bride-queen for Drimay Kunden.

With her heart full of love, she bowed and respectfully spoke this praise to the prince:

"Stainless one, like the Buddhas, you manifest purity. Your virtues are incomprehensible. Glorious one, you possess a wealth of pleasures inconceivable. As if coming into possession of the wish-fulfilling jewel, all my desires are fulfilled through you. Now that I have met the prince, universal monarch, who has rule over nature, Zangmo is happy and her heart floods with bliss."

The prince looked lovingly at Zangmo and said:

"Unchanging absolute beauty, you are the likeness of a goddess performing a blissful dance and sweetly singing lovely melody. Seeing your goodness fills my heart with joy and contentment. We are brought together by the power of prayer. Be content and enjoy the glories of pleasure and happiness."

The prince and his wife lived in the palace and devoted themselves to Dharma practice. Over time, three children were born to them. The eldest prince was named Lekden,[14] the middle prince, Lekpal,[15] and the youngest, a girl, was called Lekdzema.[16] At each of these births there was great celebration and spiritual rites were performed.

One day the prince and a group of ministers went to the flower garden to admire the beauty there. Many poor people had gathered at the palace gates for a glimpse of the prince. They stared at him woefully, like sheep in a slaughter yard. The prince was greatly saddened by their condition and said, "Father-deity, the Great Compassionate One, please hear me." Heaving a deep sigh, he went into the palace and lay down on his bed. Disconsolate and without any appetite, he incessantly recited the mantra, "Om Mani Peme Hung Hri!"

Seeing his state, the Father-King approached and said,

"Drimay Kunden, totally accomplished splendor of virtue, this Samling[17] is the sacred abode of joy, the dreamlike garden of a palace of pleasure. Here you may enjoy all the joys of the senses in their fullness. What is it that causes your overwhelming sorrow? Speak plainly, do not conceal your feelings from me."

The son replied to his father:

"O royal one, as powerful as a deity, my only father, hear me. Kye ma! Looking upon the nature of things, the suffering of samsara is universal

to all; none are spared. If one reflects only on the situation as it is, there is more than sufficient cause for sadness to arise. As a blind person pursued in darkness by the frightening forces of karma falls into the abyss, beings in the six realms are born only to plummet from the heights of birth to old age, sickness, and death. When they are rescued from this fall, my sufferings will be eased."

Thus he spoke.

His father spoke:

"Listen, O Drimay Kunden, the sufferings of all beings arise from their actions. Your sorrow gains nothing. Drimay Kunden, rest in the glories of your pleasure and bliss. If you defy my words, negative karma will increase. This is my view. If I am wrong, this will weigh heavily on me."

The prince answered:

"My only father, ruler of men, pay heed to me! I have looked beyond the palace gates, and I have seen the suffering of beings. If these poor unfortunates, deprived of wealth, were helped even more by your generosity, my suffering would be greatly eased."

To this the king replied:

"My Drimay Kunden, All-Accomplished Glorious One, you are my sole concern. My only son, whatever you wish shall be done. Abandon your sorrow." With these words, he gave his son the keys to his great treasuries, saying, "All my wealth is yours. Use it as you wish."

The prince then collected the kingdom's great treasures and wealth and piled them in a vast heap. Calling everyone to the palace, he let loose a rain of gifts. While doing this, he asked those present to recite the mantra, *"Om Mani Peme Hung Hri!"* By this activity, they were all released from poverty's sorrow.

At that time in the uncivilized country, Jema Shingdrung, the king Shingtri Tsenpo developed a negative attitude and, gathering his followers, said,

"Hear me, my people! In the capital city of Bheta, the so-called Prince Drimay Kunden has vowed to dispense his wealth impartially to all. As I have heard, everyone is talking about this. At this timely moment, who will go to beg his wish-fulfilling jewel? To him who vows to do this for me I give half my kingdom."

So he spoke.

The king's followers considered this offer. Some thought it was by no means certain that the gem would be given; in fact, many felt that to request

the gem could endanger their lives, so none volunteered for the task.

At that moment, an old Brahmin so ancient he had not a single tooth, stood and spoke: "Your majesty, I will go and do this!" The king then ordered shoes and traveling clothes and other provisions for him for the journey.

So the Brahmin, traversing many mountains and valleys, finally arrived in Bheta. There he crouched outside the palace gate, resting his head in his hands, his eyes full of tears. A minister of the court passed by, and he asked: "Old man, where do you come from, and what do you wish?"

The Brahmin replied: "From Jema Shingdrung I come to beg food and supplies from Prince Drimay Kunden."

The minister brought this request to the prince. Drimay Kunden was delighted to hear this, and came to the palace gate. "Kye, my friend," he said, "you have come on a very long journey. Having crossed so many distant mountains and valleys, your body must be weary, perhaps even exhausted. To ease your discomfort you may have whatever you wish. Only say what you need and I will grant it to you," he said.

The Brahmin cast many tears from his eyes, and clasping his hands in supplication he whined:

"Singular eye of all beings, countless in number! My country is Jema Shingdrung, and my king, Shingtri Tsenpo, has died after a three-year stomach ailment. Since then the kingdom and its subjects have degenerated. I am one of them, known as Brahmin of Wisdom. At home my starving children and relatives surround me, as emaciated as hungry ghosts. In daytime there is no food or drink for them. At night, without blankets, they huddle naked. You who love all without limit, you who give to all without bias, aid me, an unfortunate, starving Brahmin! Please grant me the gift I desire. O great Drimay Kunden, Prince of Bheta, in thanks I vow to recite the mantra 'OM MANI PEME HUNG' until death."

Thus he begged.

Then the prince brought the Brahmin to the treasury and offered him limitless wealth, including jewels precious and rare, even the famed Sampel gem, which increases whatever one wishes. The Brahmin responded:

"Great Prince, listen. I did not come to request these riches. I came to request the wish-fulfilling jewel, the jewel which even conquers enemy armies and is possessed by you, Prince Drimay Kunden, King of the Dharma." Thus he spoke.

The prince replied:

"Brahmin named Wisdom, whom I love, please hear me. My father has not given this precious wish-fulfilling jewel to me. Even if I ask, he will not do so. If one gives away those things that belong to another, much trouble will arise. Therefore please accept these jewels that have been given to me and forego your request for this wish-fulfilling jewel."

The Brahmin answered,

"Prince, listen to me! I came here hearing of your fame for gift-giving and I have experienced great hardship on the long journey. If this is the fruit of my wishes, I can no longer hope. If you cannot give up your ties to the wish-fulfilling jewel, then your pretense of nonattachment in giving anything desired is clearly a fraud. Kye Ma! If this demonstrates your commitment to giving, I had better return to my country. If you do not give me the wish-fulfilling jewel, then take back the others. I don't want them!"

He became angry and left.

The Brahmin was leaving angrily when the Prince followed and said:

"Friend, do not be of contrary mind! Maintain a compassionate view while you hear me. This is how the wish-fulfilling jewel was obtained: the white Naga Queen of the deep ocean offered the gem to the Buddha of Boundless Light.[18] This Buddha presented the jewel to my father, but this king who rules over men has not given it to me. The firmly flourishing state of the kingdom depends on this jewel. The king's great treasury is the result of its power; the three thousand ministers came from this; the country obtains its wealth, glory, and happiness from this; this precious jewel satisfies all desire. Enemy armies are subjugated by it also. For these reasons, it is the most rare jewel on this earth and throughout the three thousand universes.

"Nevertheless, even if, in giving charity I were to endanger my life, generosity is the path of Dharma. Therefore Brahmin of Wisdom, I give it to you."

Having said this, he put the jewel in a cornelian casket decorated with precious stones, saying,

"Please arise, great Wisdom Brahmin, and mount this young and power-ful elephant. Quickly take the great treasure that fulfills all wishes and destroys the armies of enemies. If my father learns of this he will pursue you and seize this jewel and your elephant mount. Furthermore, you will lose your life. Abandon laziness now and apply yourself to the path of diligence to accomplish the great goal,[19] both for yourself and for others."

The Brahmin responded:

"Son of the victorious king! Remember well, you are the object of refuge
for all beings of the three realms. You possess the emanation body of
all the Buddhas of the three times, those who are gone on to bliss. You
lead the beings of the three states of transmigratory existence that are
on the path of liberation. You are best qualified to cause the teaching
of the Buddha to blaze like the rays of the sun. You are the ship able
to cross the great flood of samsara, an army to conquer the six realms
of existence. I prostrate to you, heroic prince."

So the Brahmin praised Drimay Kunden and, putting the jewel in the
casket atop the elephant, he set upon his way. The prince prayed:

"Buddhas and sons of the victorious ones of the ten directions, please
listen to me! In order that I may satisfy the wishes and needs of
all beings and perfect the mahayana practice of generosity, may the
wish-fulfilling jewel not be stolen. May it indeed arrive to benefit the
uncivilized desert kingdom."

Thus he prayed, and returned to the palace.

When the Brahmin arrived home, he offered the jewel to his king, who

was very pleased. He gave lavish gifts to the Brahmin, and they celebrated the arrival of the jewel and enthroned it.

A month passed, and the king of Bheta, his countrymen and courtiers noticed that the wish-fulfilling jewel was missing, and its loss troubled them greatly as they gathered and discussed this event. Then the evil minister, Taradzay, went to the king, the father, and spoke:

"O mighty ruler, hear me! I have seen with my own eye that your son has given the sovereign's wish-fulfilling jewel without hesitation to our enemy. If you do not believe me, look into the treasury and see for yourself. What benefit is a son to you if you are without this gem? Isn't it right to impose justice upon him?"

Thus he spoke, and the king replied,

"Is this report really true? All rumors are half-true and half-false. There is ample time to question anew and arrive at the truth. Do not lie, minister, nor resort to slander. This jewel could not have been given to the enemy."

Taradzay answered:

"In fact it was given to a Brahmin barbarian. However, if you do not believe what you hear, it is all the same to me. I will not interfere with your heir's generosity."

Having thus spoken, he angrily departed. The king's mind was deeply affected by these words, and as though a violent poison deranged him, a black pallor covered his face.

The next morning at sunrise the king went to his son who, upon seeing him, bowed his head to the earth. The king spoke:

"This great precious treasure which grants all wishes emanates from the body of Amitabha. My radiant stainless omnipotent one, realizing your glorious nature, tell me the truth! Son of my body, the king, shedding light on nine million cities, did you give my enemy that precious treasure, provider of wealth to my lineage? Explain this well, Drimay Kunden."

Thus he addressed him, and the prince prostrated with palms joined before his father, but was unable to speak. Once more the father addressed him,

"Of all that I rule, ninety-two thousand great cities, sixty feudal states and three thousand ministers, five hundred jewels which fulfill desires, gold, silver, and countless precious objects in many treasure stores, nothing compares with the precious wish-fulfilling jewel. Nevertheless,

could it have been given to the enemy?"

The prince thought there was nothing to do but speak the truth, and he said,

"Please consider me, O great lord king! A person came to me suffering from a long journey, a person without wealth, with meager food and clothes. It is true I have given the jewel that you seek to a poor human suffering hunger and thirst, to a foreign Brahmin. I beg you do not scorn me."

Thus he spoke, and the king, his father, fell down unconscious. All the queens also suffered greatly.

After a while, having revived, the King said,

"In the northern kingdom known as Shing Bhi, renowned for five esteemed qualities is a king called Ngadra, a very powerful and superior ruler; yet he does not own a jewel of this rarity. In the south is the Southern Dzamling continent of sparkling gems ruled by one called Dragpa Thamay. His power is great, yet he does not hold the like of what I lost. Indra Bodhi, whose might is strong, rules the central continent Beru Indra Kosha, yet he does not keep that mighty gem. It was the precious vessel of my priceless trove. O you, evil enemy, because of you we are condemned to be without it, the source of my victories over my outer enemies. Now my kingdom is cast to the wind!"

Drimay Kunden answered,

"O lord and ruler over mankind, my only father, please hear me. I am wholly devoted to the path of compassion, and I have vowed to offer whatever may be wished to others. If someone begged for my sons and daughter, I would give them; I would even give my life. Father, it were better if you were less attached to riches."

Thus he spoke.

The father answered:

"In the past when this kingdom housed the precious gem, the kingdom rested mighty and at peace. Now without the like of the jewel, my dominion will be lost to enemies. You must be an enemy from a former life to have done what you have done! You went on with this without my permission and without seeking advice from your mother. Why is it you have given my enemy this extraordinary gem?"

Thus the king spoke, and again the son answered:

"Lord of the gods, my only father, hear me! You and I have made a previous commitment to provide compassionate gifts to all suffering and

needy beings, even the sons and daughter of my own body. I would, likewise, even give my life as well as the gift of the jewel that fulfills desires. Haven't I made this clear to you?"

Thus he spoke.

Again the father said:

"We agreed it was suitable to give the increasing Sampel gem, as well as silver, gold, copper, iron, vast hoards of grain, and also elephants, horses, and herds of water buffalo. All these we decided to give. But we did not agree that your life and the precious wish-fulfilling gem were to be given as charity to others."

Thus he spoke.

The son answered,

"My only father, great king, please hear me! The bee with effort collects honey, but the fruit of such work is without great outcome. Though you, my father, put great significance in wealth, riches bound with greed are without great virtue. The king who holds the treasures of three thousand universes takes with him not a penny when he leaves this world for the next. If even he departs the world with empty hands, isn't it deluded to attach such value to possessions? It would be better, Father, to be less attached to wealth. To the mind clinging like a miser to the wish-fulfilling gem, it will never return."

Thus he spoke.

The father said:

"Enemy of a former lifetime disguised as my son, this giving of the wish-fulfilling gem is like the risen sun, forever doomed to set and bring on night. My realm is blown away on the wind. Kye ma! Kye hu! Behold this misfortune!"

Thus he spoke.

The son answered his father,

"If one gives up self-clinging, loves all, and stands apart from ego's covetous possession, the joyful sun will rise, accomplishing desirable ends for oneself and others. Then also the sunrise of happiness takes place, for spiritual practice alone will suffice."

Thus he answered, and the father replied,

"Though I took you as my son and raised you lovingly, your evil intentions have emptied the kingdom. Now that I am without the wish-fulfilling jewel, as my enemy you are useless to me. I will put you to trial." Thus he spoke, and Prince Drimay Kunden was put into the hands

of executioners. These butchers took him and stripped him naked, his hands tied up against his back. With a noose on his neck they led him in a circle around the palace.

The queen of this prince, Menday Zangmo, followed after with her three children. She pulled at her hair and her eyes filled with tears expressing her woe:

"Kye hu! Kye hu! Great is my anguish to see my glorious Drimay Kunden suffering the torments of hell while still alive. Why don't the legions of devas come? May all the Buddhas be witness and look upon this faultless prince with compassion. The merciless action of the ignorant king and his ministers and retinue created this torment for him who is totally devoted to the path of compassion. The king has chosen between his son and his wealth, and wealth has triumphed over his own heir. If events continue in this way, the natural and proper way of things will be turned on its head. Consider this and realize that this prince should be treated with respect.

"How are these actions possible? Even to one's enemy one would not do this. Mighty gods and lords of nature, lords of great power on earth and mighty men, look upon these children and their mother! Is there not one with the skill to rescue us? If he exists, come quickly, and we shall return the boon forthwith. Kye hu! Kye hu! That I have seen such suffering! It is a torment to think on this and feel it in one's heart. It were better to die than to have seen what I have seen."

Having spoken thus, she followed after Drimay Kunden.

The executioners were armed with many weapons: bows, arrows, swords, and spears. They rode elephants and sounded trumpets, and their sight frightened all who looked. Some led the prince; some drove him from behind. In daylight they circled him around the palace for all to see; at night they threw him into a black pit.

The people of the city gathered and were deeply saddened by all this, but Zangmo and her children were overwhelmed by suffering. Their eyes filled with tears, they beat their fists upon their breasts, and cried out in voices wracked with sorrow:

"The stainless omnipotent one who shows the path of virtue has been a most compassionate and loving father to those who are the poorest and most hungry. Whatever was desired, he satisfied by gifts of generosity. Yet today, in place of the ripening of generosity's fruit, he is beset by wrathful vengeance. The merit of his wife and children must

be exhausted."

Having spoken, Menday Zangmo uttered a great and anguished cry.

Then the king called in the ministers who counseled his decisions and said:

"Ministers all, hear me! The prince has irresponsibly given the wish-fulfilling jewel to an enemy. Having witnessed such inappropriate behavior, what punishment do you think should be given? Consider this very carefully."

Thus he spoke.

Then some of the ministers responded, "Even if he is the prince, your son, yet he has committed actions that are banned by law. It is fitting he be flayed alive." Others said, "He should be hung upon a cross." Yet others, "His limbs should be severed from his body." Some said, "His body should be forced through a very small opening." Some said, "Tear out his lungs and heart!" Some said, "He should be impaled on the point of a stake." Others counseled, "It were better to kill him by bleeding him from head to foot." Others recommended, "It is better to crush entirely his flesh and bones." Still others said, "Let him be decapitated and the head displayed at the palace gate." Some even said, "Let the prince, his wife, and children be thrown to rot in a pit of human waste." All of them offered counsel, but none could come to agreement on a suitable punishment.

The father-king was disturbed by this, and he said to those ministers assembled: "You should remember that this is my son, devoted to the path of virtue. In addition, since he is by nature a bodhisattva, it would be unthinkable to kill him. You must still continue to deliberate." Thus he spoke.

Then a minister known as Dawa Zangpo, a man faithful and devoted to the Dharma, spoke:

"Kye ma! All you ministers, why have you counseled such severe punishment? The king has but one prince, his son. What will the people do without an heir apparent? The more I think on this, the more anguished I become, and would consider fleeing to the end of the earth. O King, this prince's only father, do not be of petty mind, nor pay much heed to these ill-minded ministers. Kye ma! How marvelous is this prince in this world, a Buddha's miraculous emanation he must be! His quality is inexpressible—it flies beyond thought! Drimay Kunden is a crown jewel among us.

"When he was led in circles before the palace, Menday Zangmo and her

princely children followed, and looking at his face, shed tears. Those who witnessed this, both old and young, including children, were deeply grieved. Many worthy followers would have gladly exchanged their lives to save the prince. 'When we see his state, we cannot bear to look upon him,' they said. 'Please release the prince and take our lives in his place.' O king, ministers, and courtiers, please reconsider! The law of the Mongols has taken precedence over the laws of Tibet in this matter.[20] Is it possible to strap two saddles to one horse? Having given the wish-fulfilling jewel is punishment enough. Dismiss his case, and be satisfied with sufferings he has incurred."

This was his request.

The father answered: "Bring the prince himself here."

The minister Dawa Zangpo went quickly to the palace gate, unloosed his bonds, clothed his body with soft garments, and adorned him with ornaments, saying: "O precious prince, please return now to the palace."

Drimay Kunden prepared to go, but the queen Menday Zangmo and the children thought: "The prince is being taken to his execution." Their faces were covered with tears and, clinging to him, they would not release him.

Witnessing this, the minister Dawa Zangpo became sad, and both his eyes filled with tears while his throat choked with grief. He approached the king and said:

"I have unloosed the prince's bonds and invited him to enter the palace, but princess Menday Zangmo and the princes and princess, their children, now imagine that he will never leave if he comes here, that he will in fact be murdered! I was suddenly beset by sorrow at this sight."

Thus he spoke.

The king responded: "Then all of them should be escorted here." The minister Dawa Zangpo invited the couple to the palace, and so they came.

The Prince Drimay Kunden and his wife and children made prostrations to the king and sat before him. The father said:

"My past-life enemy has disguised himself in the body of my son and given the wish-fulfilling jewel to my enemy. Thus have my treasuries been emptied. For the pleasure of my enemy I myself have been destroyed. All this is due to the woeful actions you have practiced. For this you will be exiled twelve years to the evil barren mountain region known as Hashang. Leave now—do not remain in this country."

Thus he spoke.

The prince replied:

"Please hear me, ruler of the gods, my only father! Not guiding the kingdom in the path of Dharma is a fault in the king. My father also lacks compassion in placing me in the grasp of low-caste executioners. I have been beaten at the joints of all my limbs, my skin torn from head to foot by thorny scourges. I was led by a rope back and forth like a wild horse. This group of murderers surrounded me like an enemy. Like a defeated warrior's sword I was exhibited to the crowd. Like a corpse I was stripped of my clothes and left naked. Onlookers encircled me like a sacred object. Like a stolen treasure I was buried in the ground at night. Weapons have been rained upon me as upon a common criminal. These are the miseries I have known. May none other experience them. Illusory possessions are useless to me; therefore I will leave as my father has declared. Be in good health, my parents, and may your subjects be well and happy."

Thus he spoke.

The five of them, the princely couple and their children, left immediately for their palace. There they charitably distributed what possessions remained to them as they prepared to leave for the evil Hashang Mountain.

The king and his ministers, including the king's subjects, made offerings on his departure. Sixty feudal kings each made offerings of a coin of gold. Three thousand ministers each offered a silver coin. The families of ninety thousand royal subjects offered horses, elephants, and many treasured objects. The prince generously gave away all these offerings as gifts, and leaving himself completely empty-handed, he spoke to Menday Zangmo:

"Zangmo, hear me. I am following my father's word in leaving for Hashang Mountain. You and our three children should return to Lotus Land, your father's kingdom. There, my dearest friend, you may stay in comfort. If in twelve years' time I am well, I pray then to meet the four of you and all your retinue. For now, be well."

Thus he spoke.

Menday Zangmo prostrated to the prince, and said,

"O precious prince, if you and I should separate, how shall I then return to Lotus Land? If you go by yourself to Hashang Mountain, how can we, your wife and children, stay behind? If we have earlier lived in happiness, how can we live apart in grief? My thoughts cannot encompass this. It overwhelms my mind. Please take us also wherever you go."

This was her response.

Again the prince spoke:

"You, Zangmo, should not speak so. In the joyful country of your birth, two parents live to counsel you. These three children are, furthermore, entrusted to your care. You will also have male and female servants to ease your labor. Enjoyable people will be your companions. You will sit upon a lotus seat and be clothed in pentsali.[21] If hungry, you may feast on the eight exquisite foods. If thirsty, you may drink of the endless stream of nectar. If you are melancholy, you may be soothed by song, revived by dance. At Hashang mountain there is only water and fruit for food and drink, only leaves for clothes and grass for a seat. There birds and beasts console one's sadness. By day the land is barren, by night it is filled with ghosts. It is a very terrifying place. Snow and rain fall without ceasing, day and night. You would find living there intolerable. Remain in your palace; I will return soon."

Again Menday Zangmo, taking hold of the prince's hand, replied:

"If you do not take me as your servant, I shall depart from life today. Without you, who will be my support? Please do not act as you plan; instead, take me as your servant."

Thus she spoke, and the prince again replied:

"Zangmo, listen! I am happy in my charity. If there were someone who would beg of me my wife and children, I would give those gifts. If there were someone who would ask of me even my own life, this also would I give. If these events should arise, you would only be an obstacle. So you, mother and your children, should remain."

Thus he spoke.

Again Zangmo replied:

"Great prince, listen to me now! Bring me along! I will assist you in your charity, even if you were to give the children and myself. In order to fulfill your vow, I will undertake whatever you command. Therefore, please bring us with you as your servants."

This was her answer to the prince. And Drimay Kunden accepted Zangmo and the children as his servants.

Then the great Prince Drimay Kunden went to his own mother, Gayden Zangmo, prostrated before her, and said:

"Mother who has given birth to all the buddhas of the three times, one who by her very nature is holder of the four limitless qualities[22] and the ten perfections,[23] mother who fulfills all hopes, ripens aspirations, and relieves need, greatest mother of all, listen to me here! To the enemy I have given the wish-fulfilling gem, and so the father-king

has showered me with rebuke and punishment. To the evil mountain Hashang Kemkem[24] I have been banished for twelve years—so I will go. Meanwhile, to you, my mother, may negative karmic circumstance or instantaneous cause of illness not arise. If also in that time I do not die, I pray we meet soon, son and mother."

Having spoken to his mother thus, she fainted. But after a short time, regaining her senses, she seized her son's hand as tears streamed from her eyes. She spoke:

"My Drimay Kunden, gloriously accomplished one, from the beginning I am the mother who gave birth to you and now it seems I lose my very heart in losing you. If you go to fearful Hashang mountain for twelve years, those years will weigh heavily against an old one's life. Without you, who will serve as my support? Kye Ma Hu!

"What has come over the mind of the great king that, in old age, he should part from his only son? At first, childless, we suffered misery. But by the blessing of prayer and offerings made to the Three Jewels, and by the fruit of offerings made to those in lower realms, by the blessing of the steadfast objects of refuge, a very precious son was born to me. When others spoke their mind, why did he exile you to the distant mountain? If we knew before your birth that bringing you to life would bring this karma, we would have accepted this. Perhaps the father-king has been possessed by an evil spirit."

Her son responded,

"O great mother, do not weep! All the beings in the three worlds of samsara[25] are subject to being torn away from that to which they cling. Mother, keep me present in your mind. Though it is true that I am born of your flesh and blood, it is a law of nature that all beings, once gathered, will separate. A dawn of faultlessness will yet arise from the edge of space. Eventually, all will be restored. I pray that we will meet, son and mother, in this life. But if this is not so I pray that later we will meet again in the next life in the pure land."

So he spoke to his mother. The mother all this time shed many tears, tightly clasping the hand of Drimay Kunden.

Then this thought came into his mother's mind:

"My son is going far away; I must not cry, it would not be seemly now." So with her hand she wiped away the tears and made prostrations to the deities of ten directions. She made this prayer: "Son of the Victorious One, arhats, and bodhisattvas, the four mighty protector kings, treasure

holders, god of wealth, all the classes of great dakinis, powerful guardians of this country, devas, nagas, tribes of Nojin,[26] all of you please
heed me and consider me! When my son enters upon his exile, let
it not be in error,[27] but the path of liberation! As he speedily crosses
mountain ridge and valley, may he know no weariness or exhaustion.
When he finally arrives at evil Hashang Mountain, may he find himself
a victorious palace.

"When he eats cold fruit and other gathered foodstuffs, may they enjoy
the savor of the eight supreme nectars. When in his thirst he drinks from
streams, may these become an endless flow of milk. When he resorts to
leaves to clothe himself and sits on boughs to take his rest, may these
become pentsali and the lotus seat. When vicious beasts are heard to
roar in anger, may these take on the sounds of mahayana Dharma. When
the tumultuous shout of the river is heard falling to the valley, may this
become the mantra of the six syllables. When suffering great heat in
the long deep valley, may the gods provide cooling shade.

"When remaining on the fearful mountain without the solace of human
company, may all the buddhas offer consolation. When illness strikes
the body, the result of past activities, may life-preserving medicines
spontaneously appear. Finally, wherever you abide, may you be free
from sorrow and experience great bliss. May obstacles be pacified and
favorable circumstances arise. O king's son, you, Drimay Kunden—may
the multitude of your aspirations increase in number to match those
of the wish-fulfilling tree. May the truth of my words, sprung from my
heart, enable son and mother to meet again soon."

Thus she prayed.

The princely couple and their three children, five in all, set forth for
the evil mountain Hashang. Two horses pulled the chariot of the prince. The
queen and the three children rode together in a chariot drawn by two horses.
Also in the train were three elephants to carry their possessions as they set
out upon the road. Led by the queen mother, Gayden Zangmo, a train of one
thousand five hundred queens accompanied them. So also followed King
Zangpo attended by sixty subject kings. The minister Dawa Zangpo led three
thousand ministers on the route. Finally the foremost servant, Palden, head
of the house, led the retinue of attendants. Expressing great sorrow, they
accompanied them far to send them on their way.

After crossing many plains and mountains, Drimay Kunden thought:
"This escort becomes weary."

So he said:

"My great mother and escorting queens, feudal kings, and ministers, Dawa Zangpo and Palden, all servants and attendants! You have accompanied us in kindness through many mountains and valleys. You, the best of escorts, have pleased me as if you had accompanied me upon the path of death. Having been together, we have become friendly and now, being separated, we are to follow the fate of all things composed of parts. My needs are satisfied, and I am relieved of the pangs of separation. All of you should now return to your own country.

"When home, behave according to the principles of Dharma. Remember life's impermanence and devote your life to charity. Place your trust in the Three Supreme Jewels, both now and in the future. To obtain the blessing of the guru, meditate his presence on one's crown. After praising the dakini who removes all obstacles, then make offering to the Dharma protectors. If after twelve years I remain healthy, then I shall pray to return to my dear native land and see you again. If by chance we do not meet again, may we meet in our next life in the pure land, Dewachen."

All those who had accompanied the prince on his way into exile uttered lamentations, and making many prostrations, they returned toward their homes. The queen mother Gayden Zangmo took hold of the prince's hand and spoke:

"Gloriously accomplished Drimay Kunden, by the karma of former lives, for me, your mother, you are my very heart. Now it has been torn from my breast, banished to the fearful mountain. The sun that has illuminated my life has set. Now upon whom shall I rely in my time? Your father, the king, has been influenced by the thought and the speech of an evil minister. Only such an outrageous occurrence could explain his willingness to agree to such inappropriate action. But you, my son of pristine mind, please go on your way. Do not be unhappy even for a moment, for you will occupy my thoughts.

"O my son, again and again, I will call out to you three times, 'My son!' I will call you three times, saying, 'Drimay Kunden!' Son, at that time, call me three times, saying 'Mother!' At that time, call me by name three times, saying 'Gayden Zangmo!'

"During the three summer months you will hear the roar of the blue thunder dragon.[28] At that time I will remember you, my son. I will call out to you three times, 'My son!' I will call you three times, saying, 'Drimay Kunden!' Son, at that time, call me three times, saying,

'Mother!' At that time, call me by name three times, saying, 'Gayden Zangmo!'

"In the three winter months will come the roar of chilling wind. At that time I will remember you, my son. I will call out to you three times, 'My son!' I will call three times, saying, 'Drimay Kunden!' Son, at that time, call me three times, saying, 'Mother!' At that time, call me three times by name, saying, 'Gayden Zangmo!'

"In the three spring months will come the song of the blue cuckoo. At that time, I will remember you, my son. I will call out to you three times, 'My son!' I will call three times, saying, 'Drimay Kunden!' At that time, call me three times, saying, 'Mother!' At that time, call me three times by name, saying, 'Gayden Zangmo!'

"To me, your mother, always turn your mind. I hope to be rejoined with you before my life is over, but if this is not possible, I pray to meet you on the path of liberation."

Thus speaking, she shed many tears and turned home. Later the prince's family, the five, looked back and saw their escort far away.

At a narrow mountain pass three poor beggars met them asking for alms. The prince was very pleased by this, and said:

"Though these priceless elephants are a great aid to our travels and come from the land where precious gems abound,[29] though I have great need for them, I will make gifts of them to you, O Brahmins, in order to fulfill your wish."

So speaking, he gave the elephants away.

Traveling from that place a distance of about a mile, they met five men at a place called Kalingkyida. These five poor men begged for their horses. The prince responded:

"Very good! These precious horses run as quickly as the wind, and these chariots are beautiful, adorned with garlands, but accept them with the pure motivation of my gift. May it have the strength of miraculous power."

Saying this, he gave them away.

The prince then led the way on the path, the three children following, while Menday Zangmo walked at the rear, carrying their food on her back. Presently they arrived at a place called Palgyi Samling. There they found a clear green upland pasture with pure water, pleasing to the mind, growing many flowers and surrounded by green mountains. Many animals and birds frolicked and played about them. There, under the shade of a *tala* tree, the

royal family sat down to rest by the side of a brook.

Menday Zangmo went to the stream, and after drinking some water she looked around, casting her eyes in every direction. She saw no one, however, only animals frisking and gamboling about. She was saddened by this prospect and said:

"Kye ma! Here wherever one looks, no one is to be seen. It seems we will not meet friendly people. Zangmo's mind is saddened by the sight of these animals frolicking in pleasant company. When one has recourse only to water to remove thirst, there is no security in hoarded wealth. That such events could occur never entered my mind. The cause must be the negative karma of former lifetimes."

Thus she spoke.

The prince thought:

"Zangmo is becoming unhappy in this empty valley without the comfort of people. Ahead there is still the distress of the road and many hardships, including the fear of fierce beasts, so it would be best for her to go home."

He therefore said to her:

"Listen to me, Menday Zangmo! We must travel great distances still. We will encounter the hardships of high mountains and steep valleys. There is much to fear, including wild beasts, which you will be unable to tolerate. Wouldn't it be better to go home now?"

Thus he spoke.

Zangmo prostrated to the prince and said:

"O great prince, hear me! What I said before was foolish. Whom should I rely on without you? How can I separate from you, my lord? I hold no doubt. By all means, take me with you."

After traveling further some distance, they took their rest in a green pasture. Again Zangmo was saddened, and she spoke in a voice barely audible to the prince:

"Here we are, at a place verdant with lush grass, without mankind, but where the bees dance and buzz their happy song. A chorus of many birds accompanies them. Wherever I look, I am again depressed. When the couple and their family have been exiled absolutely, does this do credit to the kingdom of Bheta?"

Having spoken, they went onward.

At a high mountain place, beautiful and laden with fruit, where animals gamboled on clean open ground, Zangmo said:

"Great one, hear me. Many bright flowers abound in this gorgeous region. The melody of the cuckoo blends with the sound of the running brook. There is plentiful fruit and the animals play and sing. Wouldn't it be right to remain here?"

Thus she spoke.

The prince answered:

"I will bear the sin of disobeying my father's command if we stay in this place and do not go on to Hashang Mountain."

Thus he spoke, and again they continued onward, but now the three children, exhausted and lame from the long trek, stopped, and so Drimay Kunden prayed:

"O gracious guru, deity and dakinis, deity of the region, please help me to fulfill my promise. Though Hashang Mountain may at this point be quickly reached if we two proceed swiftly, yet these young children cannot travel. Therefore it would be wonderful if the Evil Mountain came nearer."

As he prayed thus, the mountain moved ten miles closer.

Again they went onward, coming to a place called Lungbaden Yowaytsal. At this place they found a cheerful lotus garden. Menday Zangmo spoke to the lotus flowers:

"Water-borne body untouched by water, your buds appear to be happily smiling. By joining the hands of your petals above your crown, you respectfully move with grace."

Thus she spoke.

They traveled from there to Zangling Palgyiwo, where three poor Brahmins[30] arrived and said: "Please give us a worthy gift." Thus they spoke.

The prince said: "Where did the three of you come from? Aren't you tired?"

"Sir," one of them responded,

"We three are from Jema Serling. I am eighty-one-years old and have a young Brahmin girl for a wife. As I become older she is increasingly dissatisfied with me and has become more and more abusive. The other villagers also encourage her contradictory attitude. She has been speaking with two Brahmin women who have been telling her: 'He is an old man! A young woman like you should not be living with him.' She is very obnoxious all day long, and allows me not a moment of peace and quiet. She said to me: 'If you want to continue to live with

me, you and your two friends should go and obtain the three children of Drimay Kunden to be my servants. Then I will remain with you. If you do not do this, I will leave.' I told her the three children would not be given. She said,

'The Prince has vowed to give everything that is asked of him, so he will give his children.' Thus we have come to see you, sir."

The prince replied:

"That is all well, but these three children are too young to be used as servants, and it would be a pity to separate them from their mother."

The Brahmin answered:

"Why a pity? They will not be butchered. They will only be asked to do whatever they can do."

The prince then thought:

"I have made a vow to give to others whatever they desire. Therefore I must give away these children. But there is a danger that Menday Zangmo will not be able to let loose her attachment to them."

Therefore he said to Zangmo:

"Go find some fruit to serve our guests." Zangmo went in search of fruit. By the virtuous deity, no fruit was found nearby, which would have proved an obstacle in giving the children, and so she had to travel far.

During that time the prince took the hands of his three children and spoke to them:

"Lekpal, Lekden, and Lekdze, brothers and sister three, today marks the ending of our long time together. Having lived in a very harmonious way, we now must be separated. My affections are still very much with you. This is a sign of the impermanent nature of all aggregate elements. All the six classes of sentient beings also, having come together, will separate in the end. Brothers and sister, you three, do not be attached to your father and do not fix your thoughts on your mother. Go instead to fulfill the Brahmins' wishes. There will be a time when we will meet again."

Thus he spoke, and they were given to the Brahmins.

The three children, young as they were, and not seeing their mother, were troubled by this. Thus they delayed their departure moment by moment, and so the Brahmins tied them to a tree, pulled off their clothes, and whipped them with a thorny branch. The Prince, shedding many tears, was unable to look and covered his head with a cloth. Holding the children's hands, the Brahmins began to lead them away.

The children cried out, calling, "Mother!" Then Lekden said:

"We three, brothers and sister, please permit us to make prostrations to our father before we leave." The Brahmin responded, "That will be done." Lekden then prostrated to his father, saying:

"In order to accomplish an important vow of our only father, we accept that we children are given in charity. As our father has requested, I will agree to go. Though I am saddened at not meeting with our mother before we part, I know we are cherished kindly and are dear to our mother's heart. I hope that both our parents will remain well."

Thus speaking, he wept.

Lekpal then spoke:

"Our father has vowed to give to everyone that which they desire. If I refuse to go I would contradict his wish. Therefore to fulfill your promise, I will also go, but my mind is also saddened at not meeting with our mother before we part. Is it possible to see our parents again in this lifetime? If this is not possible, I pray that when we meet in the next life, we all walk on the path of liberation."

Thus speaking, he shed many tears.

Then Lekdzema said:

"I, Lekdze, the young peacock, am forced to leave two parents who are like the wish-fulfilling tree, and go with the low-caste Brahmins. Just as our father has commanded, I will go, but I sorely miss not meeting with the one who dearly cherished me and gave me milk, my mother. Because of this my mind is sad, but I pray that if in this life we do not meet again, surely we shall in our next lifetime."

Thus speaking, she also wept.

Then their father also let fall many tears, and said:

"Brothers and sisters, you three are my heart. I also experience the suffering of this separation, but because the generosity of gift giving is the very path of the Dharma, you three should be courageous and restrain your tears. O precious guru and great compassionate one, when these

royal children set forth on their journey, please prevent the obstacles of illness, and by the sincerity of this, my prayer, may we parents meet again with them soon."

Thus he spoke.

The Brahmins took the three children, and after traveling far they were separated, each taken by a single Brahmin to his own home.

Menday Zangmo, having gathered fruit, returned at last and said,

"The Brahmins and my three children are not here. This is because of the appearance of the Brahmins. They must have been given away."

She fell to the ground at this thought and expressed her sorrow with these words:

"Like a radiant sun are those three children, but now it is as if they are suddenly obscured by clouds. This is because of the appearance of the Brahmins. My garden has been beaten down by this sudden hailstorm. O spiritual guide, my lama guru, O yidam and dakinis, so powerful all, and you, guardian of this country, you powerful ones, all in an instant this sign of impermanence came. Why has this misfortune befallen me? These three children are my innermost heart, and now they have been torn from me while I am yet alive. O the suffering we endure, mother and children! Shouldn't the evil Brahmins be to blame for this?"

Thus speaking, she fainted away in her sorrow.

On seeing this, the king thought: "What a pity!" and sprinkled water on her face to revive her. When she awoke, the king said this to her:

"Zangmo, listen to me. Have you forgotten our two earlier commitments? When we set out for the Evil Mountain, leaving Bheta country, didn't I speak to you so: 'Benevolence is my joy. If someone requests it, I would give my child and wife, even my life I would give.' Didn't I say as much? You vowed you would not restrict me in my giving, that you too would practice the two accumulations of the bodhi path.[31] Having made that vow, it was agreed that we would go as one, but now you are overcome by sorrow. As together we passed through many mountains and plains, only you offered me comfort and companionship. I am saddened to see you overwhelmed by sorrow."

Thus speaking, the prince shed many tears.

Then Menday Zangmo, wiping away the tears of the prince with her hand, said:

"Great Prince, think of me. When the children left they did not say goodbye. I shed tears because of my love for them, not to upset you.

These beautiful children were my very heart, and now the Brahmins have scattered them. Alike of heart were these brothers and sister, and now their image comes again and again into my mind's eye. I am saddened as I think on this endlessly. But I will never go against your word, O Prince, and in order to fulfill your vow I will agree to whatever you may wish. Let us continue now. I will be your faithful servant."

Having spoken, they continued on.

Some time later they arrived in a locale covered in thick forest where there was abundant fruit. At this place Zangmo, gathering fruit, offered it to the prince. He ate some, for they were flavorful and had a pleasant texture. Holding one in his hand, he said:

"This is the very fruit of Amra, of the eight delightful flavors. Of all delicacies, these are the best. If I would meet the royal children now, I would share with them, but without them I am greatly saddened." Saying this, he looked at Zangmo and saw that she was weeping. The prince spoke thus: "Ah kyang! When talk is unguarded, anything is said. Without careful thought, anything may arise in the mind. In the exercise of awareness, doesn't all appear to be self-delusion? Zangmo, please share with me in the fruit of Amra,"

he said.

Then they traveled onward until they arrived at a vast and deep river, difficult to cross. There the prince made this prayer:

"O guru, yidam, and dakinis, compassionate ones, lords of the earth and guardians of this region, O beings of power, in witness to the truth, please create a passage through this river. If I must stay here, prevented from crossing by the current, I will violate my father's command. How can I then obtain the bodhi path in the next life? Please create a path in this river."

As he spoke the river whirled around, flowing upstream as the water dropped downstream, creating a path they could pass through. The prince thought that if the river remained parted in this way, it would be harmful to many beings, and so he said: "You, river, flow as before!" And the river returned to its former course.

Again they continued to a place called Lungden Yoway ravine where the two rulers of the devas, Brahma and Indra, emanated as two Brahmins in order to test Drimay Kunden's vow of stainless generosity to determine if it were relative or absolute. Approaching him, they said: "Your excellency, great king, please grant us a gift."

The prince thought: "It is impossible for any man to reach this place. Is this, then, the miraculous emanation of a spirit?" He responded to them: "Where are you two from? I have no possessions to give."

The Brahmins answered:

"We two have come from a region called Pawa. We are deprived of friends and servants. Please grant us your queen."

This was their request.

The prince thought:

"If I do not let Zangmo leave with them, all of my earlier gifts will be fruitless. If I do grant her to them, it is pitiful that she should travel with me such a distance only to part, yet I see no alternative."

He spoke to his wife:

"My dear Menday Zangmo, by accumulation of merit in past lives, you have won a human body. If called for, it is necessary to let go of one's body and life as a gift for the practice of Dharma. The root of Dharma is generosity. I will therefore offer your body and life in compassionate giving. We have lived together so long that this thought is unbearable to me, but this time, Zangmo, if you stay, my vow will not be fulfilled and you will not achieve the merit to experience happiness in your next life. Therefore go satisfy the wishes of the Brahmins. Regard the Brahmins and myself without distinction; consent to their requests. I will keep your memory alive, dearest, in the depths of my heart."

Thus speaking, he gave Zangmo to the Brahmins.

At that time Zangmo said:

"If you give me to the Brahmins, there will be no one to serve your needs, so please keep me."

Thus she spoke, and the prince responded:

"Zangmo, listen to me. I have made a vow to grant everything desired. Do not obstruct my charity, but help me in my practice of the two accumulations of the bodhi path. Do not be concerned for me; go attend upon the Brahmins. Thereby you will serve me as well."

This was his response.

Zangmo shed many tears, but she consented at last to go. Then the prince spoke to the Brahmins:

"Brahmins, hear me. The lady Zangmo has been my companion through many lifetimes; she comes of royal race and lineage. Both beautiful and charming, she is adept at preparing delightful meals. I do not need her—take her."

Thus he spoke, and the two Brahmins led Zangmo away.

After walking one hundred paces, they returned and, approaching the Prince, they offered Zangmo to him, saying:

"Ah Kyang! O lord of men, we have done this for amusement. It is wonderful that you have made meaningful this free and precious life. You, great lord, who have made the highest gift, are

also
one who would give up
even your own life. We prostrate to you,
generous prince."

Thus they offered praise, and from the mouth of Drimay Kunden came these words:

"Once given, I cannot take back a gift. You two should therefore lead her away."

Thus he spoke.

The two Brahmins then transformed into the bodies of the devas, Brahma and Indra, and said:

"Great king, we were testing your attachment. We do not need your queen."

This was their answer.

As they spoke they cast their eyes to the sky, and there appeared a host of devas in a vast celestial nomadic throng. This multitude of heavenly beings paid homage to the king

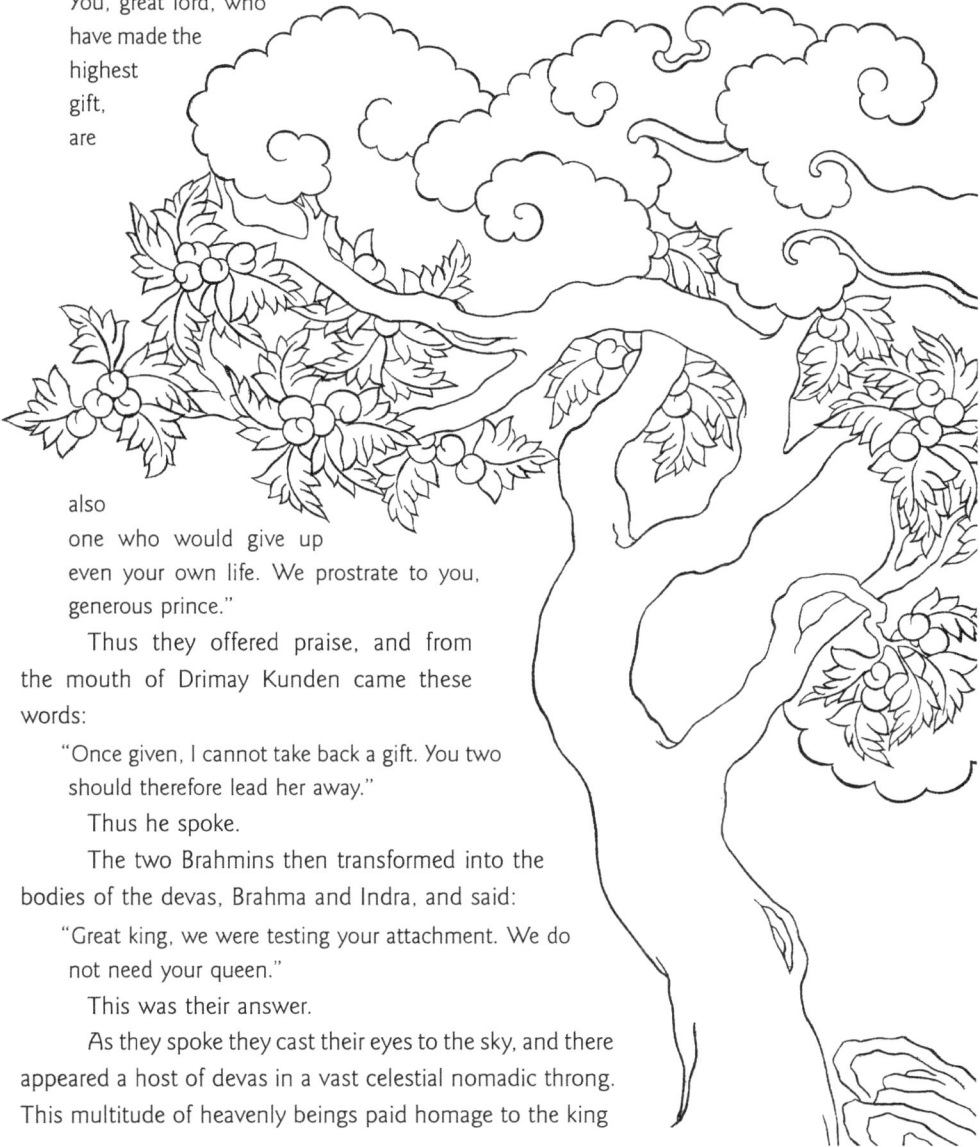

and queen. Then Indra, king of devas, made prostrations, saying:

"O precious lord, king of devas and humans, you have given up the comforts of this life for future benefit. In truth you will accomplish great profit for all and achieve supreme enlightenment. You are the marvelous light of the universe! O supreme being, to you I prostrate, unequalled in this world!"

So they spoke and then departed. The royal couple, moving onward, looked back to see the nomad encampment disappear like a rainbow.

As they continued, they met a white boy holding a crystal rosary. He said to them:

"Great king, at a distance of about two miles from here, Brahma, king of devas, will make offerings to you."

Having spoken, he disappeared. From there they went on to the banks of a large river where Brahma, exercising his miraculous power, created a huge city and there made offerings to the couple for seven days.

Then the Prince and his queen again prepared to leave, and Brahma, appearing in the form of the white boy, said:

"Great king, please remain at this place. I will provide you with housing and wealth, male and female servants to do your bidding, and you will be released from your father's punishing edict. Hashang, the evil mountain, is indeed a vile place. There vicious demons, evil spirits, and fierce animals draw near relentlessly in overwhelming numbers. It is a fearful place, a dark mountain with hostile terrain. It is not a place for you to be."

Thus he addressed them.

The Prince responded:

"By the accumulated merit of previous lives I have come into inexhaustible wealth. Your offerings to me show you also have faith in the value of pure and virtuous deeds. I have therefore accepted your gift of all desirable objects, but if I become attached to this new wealth, from this unsettled state of mind will come an increase, not of pure and virtuous acts, but gradual obscuration and grasping. If I ignore my father's word, I will be guilty of a broken vow. Therefore it is essential to leave for Hashang immediately."

As they went, the city vanished from their eyes like the fog of breath upon a mirror. Then the Prince said,

"Thus have my prayers to the Three Jewels come to bear fruit in this lifetime."

Traveling, they arrived at a depressing place, a thick forest obscuring benevolent sunlight. In the darkness they were lost and could not find their direction. Here they met a solitary yogi with blond eyebrows and mustache, his hair knotted at the crown.[32] In his hands he held a damaru and a thighbone trumpet. He said,

"You are a courageous, pious person. From which country have you come? Now where are you going? What is your name? Ten miles from here is a place called Black Mara Mountain,[33] a country of wild hills and rugged ravines. There pebbles the size of grains of salt throw shadows as long as tall trees. Poisonous trees burst into bloom. Acrid lakes cast up their waves. The cloudlike breath of snakes obscures ravines. Malevolent devils and evil phantoms, day and night, take lives. Tigers, lions, bears, and fierce beasts of all kinds, overcome by their hunger, attack and eat humans, prompted by scent. Just seeing this country gives rise to fear; even the road leading to it is fraught with unimaginable and frightening experiences."

Thus he spoke.

The Prince answered,

"I am Drimay Kunden, the Stainless Omnipotent One. My country is
Bheta, far better than this. To Hashang I go."

The yogi responded:

"Prince Drimay Kunden, many tales have I heard of your generous
almsgiving and your gift of a kingdom. Now that I see you, I have
gathered great merit. Go from here two miles to the river called Nagara;
from there to the right runs the wild beast path. Follow that track; it
will guide you correctly. May we meet in our next lives!"

So speaking, he disappeared.

From there they continued, thick forest obscuring the sun. Ferocious
ghosts and demons appeared, even in daylight. Fierce beasts ran toward them
roaring and howling. They were beset by poisonous waters and boiling waves.
At that time Menday Zangmo was frightened. Overcome with sadness, she
cried:

"E Ma! What horrible place is this? Ghosts, cannibals, and evil spirits all
appear here in daylight, and great magical and supernatural events are
seen! This must be the city of Mara, the Lord of Death. Here are tigers
and lions, fierce beasts of all sorts, bears snarling and showing their
teeth. I am greatly depressed by the roiling lakes of poisonous water,
for from here it seems impossible to escape. Now my life must be over!
O precious Lama, deity, and the Rare Supreme Jewels, please preserve
our lives, husband and wife. Lead us on our path!"

Thus she spoke.

The Prince, hearing his wife's prayer, thought, "Zangmo is very frightened." He said:

"Wrathful ghosts, spirits, and demons all, demigods and powerful earth
spirits, tigers, lions, wild boars, wolves, bears, and other fierce beasts,
heed me for a moment, please! I have realized emptiness-wisdom,
therefore I hold no grip on body or life and I know no fear, but Menday
Zangmo must be calmed. Cease your harmful and aggressive attitudes.
Act with compassion, do no harm, and remain in great peace."

Thereafter all the malevolent beings lived peacefully like groups of
long-acquainted pets, wagging their tails at the sight of their owners and
protecting them from harm. Flocks of birds wheeled in the sky, sending forth
their sweet sounding notes to welcome the newcomers. From there the couple
continued on to the snowcapped great Mara Mountain. Its lower slopes were
the color of red clay, and from its center many brooks gushed forth. At the

time of their arrival the withered trees put forth green leaves, and dry springs were replenished. Then in welcome came all the inhabitants of the district: local gods, nagas, garudas, asuras, scent-eaters, cannibal ogres, demons, and demi-gods; tigers, lions, bears, snow leopards, and eagles; foxes, wolves, and others; bulls, horses, and elephants; cranes, eagles, geese, ducks, peacocks, parrots, and sparrows, the entire family of birds and all other living beings and their kin gathered and welcomed the Prince and his queen.

As they looked toward the mountain they saw that it now faced to the south, and that the sun shone upon it early in the day and set upon it late in the evening. With harmonious sounds, clear brooks started flowing and the mellifluous songs of birds filled the air. Even the great tree of Ahna was now found there. The earth became fertile and produced many flowers, delightful, sweet-smelling, and colorful. At this place they each built a hut of dry leaves and grass. The king, his mind focused on meditative visualization combined with emptiness, remained in his hut in meditation for a long time, mindful of the mahayana teachings. At a short distance Zangmo also sat in her hut meditating, and occasionally picked the abundant fresh fruit and brought it to the Prince.

However, after some time passed, Zangmo greatly missed her children. Coming to the Prince, she said:

"Young Drimay Kunden, your state of mind is pure and peaceful; please listen to me. At this magnificent place twelve years have passed; we embarked on a six-months' journey to arrive here and we require six months to return to our home. Shouldn't we therefore prepare to leave now and return slowly?"

Thus she spoke.

The Prince answered:

"Zangmo, listen carefully to me. As prophesied by the Buddha's fore-knowledge, we have given up distraction in this tranquil, blissful forest. True practitioners of the lineage are content in this place. Our virtuous actions bring increase of merit. I shall not leave."

Having spoken, he remained in meditation.

After they spoke, Zangmo went to find fruit at the edge of the forest. There she met a colorful parrot who communicated with her, first through signs and later through speech. Zangmo addressed him:

"O beautiful bird, blessed with speech, you charm and inspire me! I am especially taken with your colorful breast plumage and your brilliant red

beak! It is a wonder to me that birds on the wing fly through space! Of sky flyers you are the most beautiful, and you are also gifted with intelligent mind. Since I have arrived at Hashang Mara Mountain, I have not found human food. O colorful, youthful, and sweet-sounding bird, so brilliant of speech, please show me a source of sweet fruit."

Thus she spoke.

The parrot jumped back and forth on the tree three times and said:

"Virtuous queen of the Prince Drimay Kunden, of youthful appearance and grace! Your complexion is soft and your body sweet-scented, blessed with the nine pleasurable signs and noble lineage. Seeing your face like a full moon, my heart was attracted and plunged to the depths of an ocean. Seeing you has so greatly pleased me, bright goddess, I will happily guide you to any fruit you may desire."

The parrot then led Menday Zangmo to the sites of the tastiest fruit, and even flew to the tree of Ahna and from there gently dropped delights to the princess waiting below.

When Menday Zangmo had enough to eat, she said:

"Winged magical bird that flies free in space, this fruit has satisfied me. Virtuous one, please maintain equanimity and treat your fellow birds with equal kindness. Since you are a kind friend, I pray to meet you again soon."

The parrot came down from the tree and accompanied the princess on the ground for eighty steps.[34] He answered:

"You of the charming goddess body and the smiling face of a radiant utpal flower, farewell! If we do not meet again, I pray to see you in my next life."

The parrot then left her and flew back into the woods. Zangmo also went on her way, returning by an unfamiliar road. There she saw a roaring, swiftly coursing river. In her mind she thought:

"E Ma! Marvelous! This river flows toward Bheta, where my children are. By this river I might communicate with them!"

With that in mind, she addressed the river:

"Pure and endless current of the primordial river, clothed in white silk with clear and melodious sound, the sweet flow of your waters is like a nectar saving the needy from hunger and thirst by your sweet sound, the flower of mountain glaciers. Please carry my message along as you flow, a gift to my three children. Say this: 'Your two parents are living and remain in good health; may you three children also be well and without troubles. O noble children, our separation has cast your two parents into misery—for so long we have been grief-stricken. Though we are not apart in mind, our separation has been intolerable and yet we have helplessly accepted it. When parents and children are divided and in different countries for so long, they are truly disheartened. Yet twelve years will soon have passed quickly. Soon we shall meet."

This was the message she sent.

A few days later, the three royal children set out to find firewood near the river, and from its sound they heard their mother's message. Missing their parents dearly, the message made them cry. The Brahmin's wife said to them: "Though you were told, you have not yet collected any wood. What have you been doing all this time?" Then she punished them severely.

With her mind saddened again, Princess Lekdzema went up the steep slope of a nearby mountain to gather wood. There she saw flying high an Indian cuckoo. The sorrowful girl, missing her parents deeply, said: "The cuckoo's song of Kyu-ru-ru is pleasing to my ears. The soaring bird brings me happiness." Then to Kala, the cuckoo, she said:

"I am so lonely; please land in front of me. Toward Mara Mountain are you going? You are a great bird for flying! Lady Kala, please deliver a message to my two dear parents on your way. Tell them I hope they are happy and in good health. Tell them I hope they continue undiscouraged on the path of Dharma. We are well—the four elements have not harmed us and illness has not weakened us, but we are suffering the difficulties of being separated from our parents. The sadness of your absence makes the days and nights seem endless. We are servants here, and the happiness of our sort is not great, but we are not badly treated by our Brahmin masters. We have heard the message that we will soon be gathering if you have the power and strength to meet us. Please keep us in your mind and come quickly."

This was her message to the bird.

Shortly after sunrise the next morning a cuckoo came and landed on a tree before the prince and his queen. It repeated the message of the princess. The parents were quite saddened by it and shed many tears. From their tears there sprang a lake, and in the center of the lake a tree of sandalwood grew with golden roots and leaves of turquoise. From that tree a thousand flowers bloomed and on each flower sat a Buddha. Each Buddha was an emanation of Chenrezig. Seeing this, the royal couple performed many prostrations and voiced praise. Thus the prince and his queen made prayer.

Menday Zangmo, sorely missing her children, made prostration to the king and said:

"O wise king, hear me! Here at this sacred spot twelve years have passed. For six months we traveled to come here and for six months we will travel to go home; all in all, that is thirteen years, your father's edict. Let us return to our home country. The three children and I are one in this—having recalled our home, we must reunite. Please hear this with kindness in your heart for me and prepare to leave."

And she wept.

The Prince thought, "Zangmo is very upset and worthy of compassion." He said to her: "Please do not shed tears. We two shall go now." He then rose from his seat of meditation and made ready to leave. The local devas, nagas, asuras, creatures from all around, and flocks of birds assembled, each in its own voice and together in chorus begging the king to remain while shedding many tears.

The king was aware in his heart of the pitiful state of these spirits and creatures, and so with his right hand he made the mudra of refuge, and spoke:

"Demons, ghosts, evil spirits, asuras, scent-eaters, and with you also all the living creatures here! For many lifetimes you have been parents and known love for your children. Also, you try to do what is best for your friends. Today our longtime companionship comes to an end; all beings of the three realms are subject to impermanence and separation. All of you have much faith in the Dharma, I know. Therefore, you must not harm each other. Remain pleasantly among each other, like a family of friends. If we do not meet in this lifetime, may we meet in the next!"

Thus he spoke, and the prince and his queen then set forth.

All the beings of the mountain were deeply saddened. They accompanied the royal couple a long distance, then finally and unhappily they returned to Hashang.

The mother and father continued on their journey until they arrived at a place called Gathering of Luminous Wind, and there a blind Brahmin approached them, made obeisance, and asked for alms. He said: "O king, hear me great sir! Please give your eyes to me."

Drimay Kunden was pleased to hear the Brahmin's request, and he immediately sat in meditation posture with crossed legs. "Now the fulfillment of my generosity is complete," he thought, and at once he addressed the beautiful Menday Zangmo:

"Glorious and joyful lady, hear me! Do not be attached to me. The culmination of my generosity is now at hand! I am attached to nothing;

samsara is without beginning and without end. As a result I have obtained my body, but time has gone by in essentially meaningless activity. At this moment the essence of meaningful activity shall be realized!"

His right hand held a very sharp knife, and his left hand held open his eyelids. The blood flowed out as he put the sharp blade in.

Seeing this, Menday Zangmo cried aloud in unbearable anguish and reached out to restrain his hand. The Prince said:

"Zangmo, do not do this, for this act is not loving but hostile to me. As a result obstacles could be set in our path that will prevent us for eons from meeting again. So please do not interfere with my kindness; remain quiet."

He then put the knife to his eyes once again, removing them both. Zangmo, in viewing the unbearable sight, fell down to the ground in a swoon. The king, holding his two eyes in his palms, placed them with his own hands into the Brahmin's empty sockets.

He spoke:

"Hear me well, Brahmin, good man that you are. You are happy to see, for two eyes were given you. Completing my purpose, may you view the three realms. Though I have not eyes myself, may I be guided by the vision of the Dharma. Removing the darkness of ignorance, may it shine with the clarity of the lamp of liberation. So the goal of my kindness is also complete."

And he sat silently in luminous meditation.

Then the formerly blind Brahmin realized he could see wherever he looked, and making obeisance he said:

"Great kindness goes with your lineage, O mighty king's son! Everything desired is sated by the gift of the compassionate one. The brilliant light of your lamp removes the world's darkness. In the three universes you are incomparable. You have shown much kindness to all beings in general, but for this old Brahmin in particular you have removed much negative karma. To the prince of compassion I make praise and obeisance."

Having said this, he returned to the country of Bheta.

On his return, the townspeople gathered about him and asked: "Where have you obtained your eyes? How was your sight restored?"

The Brahmin replied, "These are the eyes of Drimay Kunden, the Stainless Omnipotent One. I begged them of him."

Present at that time were Drimay Kunden's father and his mother Gayden Zangmo, and their courtly attendants and servants. Everyone was amazed at this news, and so the minister Dawa Zangpo went with servants and representatives of the court to receive Drimay Kunden.

After considerable time, the Prince's wife Menday Zangmo awoke from her faint, arose and looked at Drimay Kunden. He was still sitting cross-legged in the meditation posture, his face and the front of his clothing covered with blood. At the sight of this, Menday Zangmo again cried and said:

> "E Ma! At the fearful demon mountain, Hashang, we have spent twelve years. At last I thought we would be returning home to be reunited with our dear ones. In my mind, joy and immeasurable happiness had arisen. Instead, all my efforts and anticipation have been meaningless. Ah tse ma! Kyi hu kyi hu! This is the fruit of my efforts!"

This she cried in a very loud voice, and many tears fell from her eyes.

The prince said:

> "Zangmo, do not grieve! Put your efforts into the practice of Dharma. Generations of life in the endless cycle of existence from the very beginning of time, including even our present human birth, have all been spent pointlessly. This time it is important to seize the meaning of our fruitful activities. Zangmo, do not be miserable. Let us go on; you lead the way."

Zangmo took the hand of the prince to guide the way, and they set forth. Eventually they arrived at a place called Duwa Hari. There they rested under the shade of a tree. Soon the minister Dawa Zangpo arrived before them, and to the prince he made prostrations with folded hands, saying,

> "O Drimay Kunden, I, as minister, make a humble request. Your great father, the king, has sent us his ministers leading a group suitable for a king's escort. The queen mother herself has come, leading a group of others like herself, queens also. From sixty tributary kingdoms have come three thousand royal officers with their subjects and attendants, totaling ninety-two thousand—all your loyal subjects, all respectfully inviting you to return with them to Bheta. Kye! Knowledgeable one, your tremendous effort is amazing; glorious ocean-like knowledge, holding all of us in your kindness, please come to Bheta. With this message I have been sent to greet you, sir."

Thus he spoke and shed tears.

The prince placed his hand on the crown of Dawa Zangmo's head and said:

"Have you really come, Dazang?[35] Have you come with so large a retinue? Though I am nearly dead, yet I am still alive. Ah! But is this a joke? Listen, Dazang, is the kingdom of Bheta well? Are my parents and all their subjects in good health? If your invitation is sincere, then let us set forth."

The minister Dawa Zangpo and Menday Zangmo took the prince's right and left hand and they proceeded. But again on the roadside the prince stopped and rested, for so much blood had come from his eyes. He was very near death at this time.

The prince spoke these words:

"Now the fulfillment of my generosity is complete. My dear one, Menday Zangmo, glorious joy to me, and you also, Dawa Zangpo, return together to the country of Bheta. Once there, act in harmony with the Dharma. I will leave for another realm, a spiritual sphere."

And he sat on the ground cross-legged in meditation.

Then the great Buddhist practitioner thought:

"May the Buddha's activities of teaching and helping suffering beings attain a state of happiness be fulfilled."

With this thought, he began to pass away, and Buddhas from the ten directions appeared in the sky in front of Drimay Kunden, and on the crown of his head they placed their hands and empowered the king to pray:

"Buddhas of the ten directions who have passed on into never-ending bliss, please include me in your thoughts. In order to alleviate Menday Zangmo's misery and to fulfill Dawa Zangpo's wish, may my two eyes be returned to me even clearer than before."

As he spoke, his eyes were instantly restored with more perfect vision than before.

The retinue with the king and queen proceeded to Palgyi Samling, where on the outskirts of the country the king Jema Shingdrung made invitation to Prince Drimay Kunden, his mother, his wife, and their attendants, and offered him the wish-fulfilling jewel, the fabulous cintamani once again, along with many other valuable gems, and said:

"I was the cause of your long exile to Hashang Mountain. Now I confess my crime and beg your forgiveness, and I offer my kingdom and all my subjects to you. I also plead with you to lead me out of samsara."

The king made prostrations and circumambulated Drimay Kunden many times. The prince graciously accepted Jema Shingdrung's requests, and

thus the enemy of his father came under his sway.

As they continued on their way, they met the three Brahmins of Chema Serling who brought with them the three royal children of Drimay Kunden. The Brahmins said,

"These children have been very useful to us, but now we offer them as an act of generosity, remembering the prince's favor to us. For this reason we have come."

Then they returned the three children to the royal couple.

Drimay Kunden responded,

"That which I have given I do not take back. You three should therefore take them, and whatever work you are able to find you should let them do."

Hearing this, Menday Zangmo prostrated herself to the prince and said:

"Great prince, please hear me! These two boys and this girl came out of my body. For twelve years they have been given in service to the Brahmins, yet they are as rare as the Udumbara flower. More precious than precious are these boys and this girl. Of royal lineage they are; in their plight as servants they experienced unimaginable and unbearable suffering."

Thus she spoke, and she shed many tears.

The prince understood that Zangmo spoke the truth. He had pity, and he said:

"Do not weep, Zangmo, supremely beautiful glory of my joy, listen to me. I will bargain for the little brothers and the sister."

He spoke to the Brahmins:

"Kye ma! You three Brahmins, come back to Bheta with us. I will use my wealth to buy the children from you."

And again they set forth.

At the frontier region of Bheta, at a distance of twenty-four miles, a procession of royal ministers and commoners made offerings to the royal company, welcoming them as they proceeded along their course. The prince's father came fourteen miles along the road to meet them from his Lotus Palace in Bheta. On his way there was a city, Nangwa Wü, ablaze with light. The road was auspiciously decorated with umbrellas, victory banners, huge fans, yak-tail fly whisks, flower garlands, tents, musical sounds, cymbals, clouds of incense offerings, singers and dancers, stringed instruments, small and large bells, drums, flutes, and great horns. All of these were making music as the

streets of the city filled with the crowd welcoming Drimay Kunden home.

It was at that time that Drimay Kunden and Menday Zangmo arrived with their three royal children and the Brahmins in the city of Nangwa Wü under the dazzling lights of the city. In that bright city light, Kuntsig, a king from a nearby country, also arrived and made prostrations and many offerings to the royal couple and their entire retinue. He said:

"The sun which sets in the west each day arises likewise in the east. You, noble king, like a loving parent to all beings, have in your compassionate generosity gone to the end of the road on Demon Mountain, and now you have returned here. Your kindness has been shown to all types of sentient beings. We, your followers, have been freed from misery, and you, Drimay Kunden, have fulfilled the meaning of your name.

"You have offered your life, your children, and even your eyes to those who have only requested them. Your father should have been without regret when, without desire, you gave the wish-fulfilling jewel to his enemy. You, a sage of the mighty mountain of teachings, bear the glorious banner of victory, sustainer of men! You are modest but famous, O Stainless One! From your abode, the glorious palace of joyful bliss, you lead your realm according to the principles of Dharma. When I go beyond this life, in the next may I be a follower of yours reborn, your disciple again! This prayer I make one-pointedly.[36] May it be auspicious!"

Thus he spoke.

As they proceeded further, many other rulers of minor kingdoms also came with their retinues to make prostrations and to circumambulate the prince. The King of Gold and all his followers each presented Drimay Kunden with a single gold coin. The King Excellent and Reasonable and his followers offered silver coins. There also came others, country folk, people from nearby kingdoms, servants and householders, all of them bearing offerings of gold, silver, lapis lazuli, sun-crystal, golden nuggets, many jewels, and all kinds of valuable objects.

At the town called Paltsik Metok, the prince at last met with his father, the king. When they met, Prince Drimay Kunden and all his retinue, including the royal children, made prostrations to the father-king. Drimay Kunden took his father's hand and shed many tears.

His father said:

"Father and son thus meet again auspiciously. There is reason to weep."

And the father-king and the mother Menday Zangmo poured forth tears.

Finally all took their seats, and the prince's father, Earth Protector, spoke to the three royal children: "Come and sit on grandfather's knee, you children of my own heart!"

But although he said this, the three children hesitated to approach, and the father-king asked why they did not come to him. The young Lekden said:

"The fruit of the tree of supreme knowledge has fallen into the ocean and been eaten by hoards of Nagas. This has happened even though I am the son of a glorious noble family. By the edict of exile we were brought to the outskirts of Hashang Mountain. There we entered the long narrow path that took us into the lonely, barren valley. Our stainless father gave us to three Brahmins. I, Lekpal, and Lekdzema, we three brothers and sister from our mother's body, were given as gifts. We worked hard for each of these Brahmins; we ate dirty food and wore rank clothing. Thus we have been contaminated, and now our minds are confused. We do not wish to soil you, great king, therefore we shall not climb upon your knee, grandfather, nor shall we sit in our father's lap."

Thus he spoke.

The three royal children were bathed in a precious vessel filled with perfumed water, and new clothing was provided for them.[37] To the three Brahmins, five hundred gold coins were given for the ransom of Lekden, five hundred silver coins were paid for Lekpal's ransom, and three hundred elephants were given for Lekdzema's price. At last the three Brahmins, amply provided for their journey, returned to their country.

Then Drimay Kunden said to his father:

"Lord of men, my only father, please consider what I say. You are a man of glorious merit, O Earth Protector. As your command of exile was issued, I did accept it, traveling a long road and oppressed by heat. To a fearful mountain we went, and were molested by the terrifying activities of raging animals, malicious goblins and demons, as well as spiteful demi-gods and others. Our clothes were made of leaves and we lay upon grass mats. Fruit was our only food, cold water our sole drink. Birds and wild animals consoled us in times of sadness. Because of our desire for worldly possessions I experienced hardships such as these. May other humans never know this pain!

"By giving my father's wish-fulfilling jewel, and later by the gift of my eyes, may this bring my generosity to fruition. By the collective force of my virtue and generosity, may all sentient beings without exception

achieve true happiness, particularly you, Earth Protector father-king! May all my followers and all without exception be liberated from defilements, death, and evil actions, and in the next life I pray we will all be reunited in the same mandala. For all of these, I pray my gift will result in their enlightenment."

The father spoke kindly to his son:

"You speak the truth. Because of my error in not recognizing your true nature, I condemned you for your actions and sentenced you to exile. My action was ill-considered and you suffered for it, though I and my ministers consulted on this. On the distant road when you were yet young, your children, your eyes, and other gifts you gave—horses, chariot, elephants, and possessions—all given in charity. Thus I have heard. If that is true, then I do not regret the wish-fulfilling jewel given as your gift to my enemy. Now that I know of your great generosity, immeasurable joy is aroused in me. In the past I challenged all your generous acts as faults, but now I understand and unreservedly forgive you. I confess all my former errors, and in reparation offer you the treasured stores of all my wealth. Do as you like in dispensing them as gifts."

Then the king led his son and Menday Zangmo by the hand, and the three royal children were escorted in a chariot. When they arrived at the palace gate, Drimay Kunden's mother, Gayden Zangmo, led by attendant royal women burning incense, welcomed them. The king of the gods, Indra, with his retinue of gods, showered flowers and sounded cymbals for the royal pair. Drimay Kunden and his wife made prostrations to the queen mother, Gayden Zangmo, and the royal children bowed as well.

The mother spoke to her son:

"Stainless son, hear me! Kye ma, by the power of karma, like the power of the wind, O Drimay Kunden and your wife, the many sufferings you have experienced are now overcome. Joy arises and much of my misery and distraction today are at an end. For twelve years, because of my son, I tore my hair and rivers of tears fell from my eyes. I beat my breast in sorrow and was punished by misery's fire. But the waters of enlightenment have today quenched all these flames. My sorrows are removed, my stainless son!"

Thus she spoke.

They entered the palace and took their seats. The father-king addressed his son:

"Young Drimay Kunden, accept my crown and seven precious jewels.
Especially excellent in its destruction of obstacles is this jewel also, the
gift given to my enemy. I owned it once, and by the power of merit
it has been returned. Now, with this edict of my policy of goodness,
my royal crown with its cintamani, the destroyer of armies, my gold,
silver, pearls, hoards of silk, my horses, elephants, herds of buffalo, my
principalities and fiefdoms including their courts, servants, and armies,
I give without reservation. My young one, kindly agree to rule them."

Thus he spoke.

At this time, the king placed the crown on Drimay Kunden's head and
the queen's handmaidens led him to the throne. Placed in his hand was the
golden wheel of one thousand spokes of the universal emperor and along with it
the rule of the kingdom and its feudal protectorates. His father spoke again:

"O young dearest one of immaculate mind, make use of my wealth however you please. I place in your hands my domains and followers. Keep
the golden laws of the kingdom as straight as golden ox-beams."

Thus he spoke.

Thus King Drimay Kunden was enthroned as his father's regent, and
throughout the region to a distance of forty-five paktse[38] festive celebrations

in his honor were held. Under Drimay Kunden's rule, through his merit and power, lawful behavior and prosperity flourished to a greater extent than ever before.

Then Indra, the ruler of the gods, was invited before them and spoke:

"The wish-fulfilling jewel, the destroyer of armies, was given to the enemy. For this act you were expelled by your father to the great evil mountain, experiencing terrible suffering all the while. You endured this for the sake of sentient beings, even giving your children for this purpose. You have now obtained the clearest vision and, arriving home, you rule the kingdom. An unsound kingdom bears no fruit. I pray that all beings be given the practice to obtain unsurpassable enlightenment.

"On this earth you are the light that is most bright, a universal emperor. You will pass away into the east.[39] At Potala Mountain you will be born Zangpo Gyepa, a son of the well-known Zangpo, and in that emanation will liberate many beings. So you shall further turn the wheel of Dharma and attain enlightenment.

"After one hundred million eons have passed, at a time to be known as Wöchen, your father, Glorious Earth Protector, will be born with the name Gangchen, and his activities of Dharma and government both shall flourish under his rule. The queen Gayden Zangmo after this life shall be born in the realm of Yulo,[40] where she will become a protector of beings. In her next life, Menday Zangmo will be born in the country of Singha where she shall be known as King Dayjay. These two young noble princes, your sons, in their next lives shall be born in Southern India. There the older shall be called King Dönden and the younger shall be named Prince Tingyi Paldzin. The Princess Lekdzema will be born in the country of Odyana, that of King Day. There she shall be his son and become the ruler of the great kingdom of Satasata. The great minister, Dawa Zangpo, will be born in Nenay, the son of King Kunga Zangpo.

"By his great merit, Drimay Kunden has opened the way to virtue. The fruit of his activities are such that his mother and father, his children and his wife, even the ministers and their followers have been made happy. Fully accomplished meritorious one who is stainless and omnipotent, born in the human realm in the lineage of victorious ones, this is your amazing lotus garden. Your wisdom and skillful means provide the moisture and warmth to nurture spiritual growth. In time the tree of virtue must produce its fruit. When it matures, the blooming of its

many flowers will fall in showers, spreading its sweet pollen in virtuous benefit for all. Even I shall relinquish my god's life in order to do your service. Like the very shadow which falls from your body, I hope to be as near, always with the goal of fulfilling your aims."

Instantly he disappeared.

Then Menday Zangmo addressed the king: "Why is it that such a one of beautiful body should disappear into the unseen?"

Drimay Kunden answered:

"Zangmo, do not become concerned. Hear me. The sweet song in the warbler's throat becomes silent in time, as the hollyhock vanishes like dew on autumn grass. While the yellow-clothed sun rises, it also fades in time. The rainbow in the sky is beautiful, but it does not stay for long. All of us, also, father, mother, parents with children, come together as we have for a moment, like the Ashatata flower that disappears after only a little time. Even this joyful gathering is of brief duration; after a short time of companionship we shall also part. This so-called 'present' is only a moment; this parting of our loved ones is saddening. I shall remain in this human realm one hundred thirty years, staying for the cause of benefiting sentient beings. Thus I have prayed. My two sons shall hold this symbol of my earthly glory, this jewel of regency. Please accept this decision joyfully and practice beneficial deeds for others."

Thus Drimay Kunden's regency was passed on to his sons. The King Gawaypal's daughter, an emanation of the dakini Yeshe Tsogyal, led the procession of five hundred maidens who married the two princes. Celebrations of marriage and enthronement ceremonies were elaborately performed over an area of twelve miles in breadth. The Princess Lekdzema was sent to be married to the son of Brahmin Dayjay. Afterward King Drimay Kunden, Queen Menday Zangmo, the minister Dawa Zangpo, and the ministers Drajay and Gyaldzin and their retinue went to practice meditation on the great mountain Singala.[41] The kingdom was ruled by the two princes as before.

After five years King Drimay Kunden and Queen Menday Zangmo became two lotus flowers, red and yellow, and were carried on the wind to southern India. Then the ministers returned to their own kingdom, and carried the message that the two parents had attained parinirvana. On hearing this, the two sons rejoiced greatly for the achievement of their parents, and built a thousand golden stupas in their memory.

*May all be auspicious!*

## End Notes: Introduction

1  "Lhamo, The Folk Opera of Tibet," *The Tibet Journal*, Vol. IX, No. 2, Dharamsala.
2  *Chungpo Dhonyoe and Dhondup; Drimay Kunden; Drowa Sangmo; Gyasa Bhelsa; Nangsa Wöhbum; Prince Norsang; Pema Wöbar; Sukyi Nyima; Thepa Tenpa*, and *Songtsen Gampo*. Jamyang Norbu, noted by Joanna Ross in *Lhamo: Opera from the Roof of the World* (Paljor 1995).
3  Literally "Theatre Thesis," this is the formative treatise on Indian dramatic art, attributed to Bharata Muni sometime between 200 B.C.E. and 200 C.E.
4  Warder, A.K. *Indian Kavya Literature.* 2 Vols. Delhi: Motilal Banarsidass, 1972.
5  Warder.

## End Notes: Nangsa Wohbum

1  "Homage to the guru, deity, and dakini." Tantric Buddhist Three Roots: the lama (guru), deity (yidam), and protectors (dakinis).
2  Family of the Buddha.
3  Inner psychological obstacles to enlightenment, or actual beings who wish to obstruct one's spiritual progress.
4  Supplication prayer to Buddha Shakyamuni (the historical Buddha) recited by the narrator.
5  Pure realm of Chenrezig (Sanskrit: Avalokiteshvara). Chenrezig is the spiritual patron of Tibet, a bodhisattva regarded as the personification of compassion.
6  Seed syllable associated with the visualization of Tara, the principal feminine deity in Tibetan Buddhism. She is often visualized in a retinue of twenty-one Taras of various colors surrounding the central figure of Green Tara.
7  Epithet of Tara.
8  Supernatural beings inhabiting springs, lakes, and seas, known as protectors of wealth
9  Disembodied beings nourished by odors and smoke.
10  The Buddha.
11  Symbol of the teachings of the Buddha. "Turning the wheel" refers to the action of giving those teachings.
12  A term with numerous associations in Buddhism and Hinduism. Here it refers to the teachings of the Buddha.
13  Celestial realm of Tara.
14  Past, present, and future.
15  Buddhas. "The Victorious One" is Buddha himself.
16  The Buddha, the Dharma, and the Sangha, also called "The Three Jewels".
17  Although Tibetan lunar months are usually referred to by number, there is also an animal symbol associated with each month. The Month of the Monkey is the 10th month.
18  The Tibetan calendar uses a cycle of twelve animals similar to the Chinese system in order to identify particular years.
19  "One Hundred Thousand Rays of Light."

20  Indian songbird renowned for its beautiful melodies.

21  The calf of a yak bull and domestic cow.

22  The buddhas of past, present, and future.

23  Major categories within Tibetan Buddhism. "Sutra" refers to the exoteric texts, including those common to all schools of Buddhism, as well as the mahayana teachings. "Tantra" includes the esoteric texts of the vajrayana. The statement implies that Nangsa had completely mastered the Buddhist teachings.

24  Note that sometimes the name is "Drachen" and sometimes "Drachenpa." The meaning is the same. Similar to Western custom, the text sometimes presents names in either shortened or more extended form.

25  An important feature of tantric Buddhism in which gurus transmit permission and blessing to do a specific practice.

26  A shiny grass.

27  A white scarf traditionally offered respectfully.

28  Clockwise circumambulation of sacred objects, shrines or temples.

29  A spiritual dance performed at rituals.

30  Qualities that please the five senses.

31  A common blue stone.

32  A bad omen.

33  "Bride price."

34  Her complete name.

35  Faith, virtue, a sense of shame, a fear of blame, learning, renunciation, and wisdom.

36  The five precious substances.

37  Ani can mean "aunt" or "nun." In this case, Nyimo Netso is a nun who lives at home.

38  Expressions of sorrow.

39  Spiritual followers of the great Tibetan sage Milarepa

40  According to Buddhist teachings, through the cycles of reincarnation all sentient beings have at some time been our loving mother.

41  Beings from each of the six realms: gods, jealous gods, humans, animals, hungry ghosts, and hell-beings.

42  The patron is Nangsa herself.

43  Nyingma (literally, "the ancient ones") is one of the four schools of Tibetan Buddhism. The other schools are Kagyu, Sakya, and Gelug. Bön is the native religion.

44  One of the main lineage holders of the Kagyu tradition. He was the first Tibetan in the lineage, and translated many teachings from India. He is also reknowned for being Milarepa's teacher.

45  The terms "old" and "new" refer to different historical periods of text translations from Sanskrit into Tibetan, and the practices associated with them. The implication is that he is fully educated.

46  The long version of "dzogchen," the more commonly used term. Here, the dzogchen (Great Perfection) teachings are considered to be the quintessential Buddhist teachings.

47  Barley meal.

48  Also known as "Rahula, the Great Planet," an ancient mythological planet said to cause eclipses.

49  The bardo that occurs after death.

50 Animal, hell, and hungry ghost realms.
51 In general, lha are deities or divine beings; in this case, it
   refers to protector spirits associated with Nangsa.
52 It is generally taught in Buddhism that it is not a judgmental deity that sends
   us to our next rebirth, but our own karmic accumulation. In the narrative
   context, beings in the bardo may actually experience what is described here.
53 Significant placement or gesture, often of the hands.
54 An important female deity.
55 A personal meditation deity in tantric practice.
56 A drum made by stretching leather over the inverted crown of a human skull.
57 One of the traditional ways of describing the locations where the different
   types of sentient beings live. The three are: above the ground (heavenly
   beings), on the ground (humans), and beneath the ground (nagas).
58 Gods inhabiting one of the six realms of beings in samsara.
59 Mythological winged horse.
60 Stones on which the mantra Om Mani Peme Hum has been carved or painted.
61 Buddha.
62 Nirmanakaya, sambogakaya, and dharmakaya comprise the trikaya or three
   bodies of a buddha, which is in effect a description of enlightenment itself.
63 Great vehicle, one of the major traditions in Buddhism and considered to be
   the middle path in Tibetan Buddhism. Through compassion, a practitioner is
   motivated to seek enlightenment not just for themself, but for all sentient beings.
64 A small rounded boat made of waterproof material
   stretched over a wicker or wooden frame.
65 Deity representing the quintessence of enlightened mind.
66 Used to gather residents to events.
67 A reference to buddha nature, the enlightened essence possessed by all beings.
68 The ten virtuous actions: protecting life, not stealing, proper sexual
   conduct, truthfulness, creating harmony, gentle speech, meaningful
   speech, generosity, altruistic thoughts, and right view.
69 An esoteric tantric reference to the winds and channels, features of the subtle body.
70 The practice of tonglen, whereby one meditates on exchanging oneself for others.
71 Passion and ignorance.
72 Attachment to gain, pleasure, praise, fame, and
   aversion to loss, pain, blame, and disgrace.
73 It is said that the Buddhadharma consists of 84,000 teachings.
74 A colored cloth flag imprinted with prayers.
75 Either an enemy from a past life who has come back, or
   an enemy resulting from one's negative karma.
76 The following song employs a Tibetan literary device which
   uses the thirty consonants of the Tibetan alphabet in order.
   It is not possible to convey this in translation.
77 The mantric syllable "Ah" symbolizes emptiness. It is said that the
   entire meaning of the Prajnaparamita sutras (an essential section of
   the mahayana teachings) can be expressed in this one syllable.
78 An important meditation deity.

79 Killing, stealing, sexual misconduct, lying, creating disharmony, malicious speech, gossip, envy, ill-will, and wrong view.

80 Killing one's father, killing one's mother, killing an Arhat, injuring the Buddha or one who represents the Buddha, and causing disharmony in the sangha.

81 Remorse; confession; the power of the remedy (invoking the blessings of the sources of refuge, holy beings, and so on); and commitment to avoid negative action in the future.

82 An expression of wonder.

83 A flower that only appears when the Buddha is alive on earth.

84 A jewel that grants all wishes. Well known in Tibetan Buddhism, it adorns the headdress of many Buddhist deities.

85 Beings who experience extreme hunger and thirst due to miserliness in previous lives.

86 Beings who through jealousy in previous lives are born in a godlike state characterized by constant fighting and suffering.

87 Two categories of practitioners who are motivated to transcend samsara for themselves alone, in contrast with a bodhisattva who seeks enlightenment for all sentient beings.

88 The sutrayana is considered to be the causal path to enlightenment and tantrayana is the resultant path.

89 There are six paramitas or perfections: generosity, moral discipline, patience, diligence, meditation, and wisdom.

90 The modes of behavior that bodhisattvas adopt to bring people together to guide them on the path: generosity; kind speech; creating a relaxed atmosphere by adopting a lifestyle that is egalitarian and harmonious with their students, and; discussing topics of great meaning and relevance.

91 A traditional metaphor for enlightenment.

92 Categories of tantric practice.

93 Annutara yoga tantra, a means to achieve enlightenment in one lifetime

94 The vows of empowerment in a tantric context.

95 The vase, the secret, the wisdom-knowledge, and the sacred name empowerment.

96 Protecting life, not stealing, proper sexual conduct, truthfulness, creating harmony, gentle speech, meaningful speech, generosity, altruistic thoughts, and right view.

97 Worshipping with devotion using the Three Jewels as a guide; practicing Buddhism in this life and the next; repaying the kindness of one's parents; honoring the learned; revering the noble and elderly; shunning novelty in friendship and maintaining sustained relationships; helping one's neighbors and the poor; rationally analyzing others' words and not being influenced by gossip; modeling one's behavior on a good person; avoiding extremes in one's lifestyle; repaying others' kindness and generosity; avoiding dishonesty in business; being fair with others and avoiding envy of others' wealth; shunning bad friends and unreliable people; being soft-spoken and polite, and; undertaking spiritual and political ventures with strength.

# End Notes: Drimay Kunden

1  According to the Tibetan tradition this ancient kingdom was located in Northern India or Bengal. (Khenpo Karthar Rinpoche)
2  "Gloriously Renowned Lord of Earth."
3  Channels: nadi - networks of subtle energy in the body associated with chakras.
4  The channels or nadis, along with the chakras, are features of the subtle body.
5  "Wheel" and "chakra" are expressed by the same word in Tibetan. Clearly, an esoteric inner experience difficult to express verbally.
6  A primary symbol in tantric Buddhism signifying the indestructible and unchanging nature of enlightenment.
7  The four cardinal directions, the four intermediate directions (such as southwest), and above and below.
8  Ritual objects shaped like a three-sided dagger made of bronze, iron, wood, or meteoric metal.
9  Ritual offering cake.
10  "Stainless All-Accomplished Possessor of Knowledge."
11  Linguistics, logic, technology, poetry, and philosophy.
12  The realms of desire, form, and formlessness.
13  "Lotus Land.
14  "Nature of Goodness."
15  "Glorious Goodness."
16  "Beautiful Goodness."
17  Mythical island paradise.
18  Amitabha.
19  Enlightenment.
20  Generally speaking, Tibetans considered the Mongolians barbarians with harsh laws and punishments.
21  Clothes worn by the devas in the heavenly realm.
22  Compassion, loving-kindness, joy, and equanimity.
23  The six paramitas, plus skillful means, aspiration, spiritual power, and primordial wisdom.
24  Full name of the mountain.
25  The realms of desire, form, and formlessness, a way of categorizing the beings in samsara.
26  Literally, "harm givers." However, in this context the term refers to a certain type of protective spirit.
27  In other words, "may he not abandon the spiritual path."
28  Symbol for summer.
29  India.
30  Brahmins are sometimes utilized as comic figures in Tibetan drama, as they seem to be in this instance.
31  Merit and wisdom.
32  A description of a typical wandering yogi or tantric practitioner.
33  Another name for Hashang Mountain.
34  A mark of respect and friendship.
35  A nickname and sign of affection.

*End Notes: Drimay Kunden continued*

36  Without distraction and with sincere devotion.

37  The implication is that having lived under degraded
    conditions, the children must now be cleansed.

38  Ninety miles.

39  Considered auspicious.

40  Tara's realm.

41  Ceylon.

www.ingramcontent.com/pod-product-compliance
Lightning Source LLC
Chambersburg PA
CBHW031854090426
42741CB00005B/487